30 Weird & Wonderful New Zealand Stories

30 Weird & Wonderful
New Zealand
Stories

Edited by **Barbara Else**
Illustrations by **Philip Webb**

RANDOM HOUSE
NEW ZEALAND

National Library of New Zealand Cataloguing-in-Publication Data

30 Weird and Wonderful New Zealand stories / edited by Barbara
Else; illustrated by Philip Webb.
Includes index.
ISBN 1-86941-565-5
1. Children's stories, New Zealand. [1. Science fiction. 2. Fantasy.
3. Short stories, New Zealand.] I. Else, Barbara. II. Webb, Philip.
NZ823.0876089282—dc 21

A RANDOM HOUSE BOOK
published by
Random House New Zealand
18 Poland Road, Glenfield, Auckland, New Zealand
www.randomhouse.co.nz

First published 2003. Reprinted 2003, 2005

ISBN 1 86941 565 5

Text design: Kate Greenaway
Cover illustration: Philip Webb
Cover design: Katy Yiakmis
Printed in China

Contents

Introduction

Here's a collection of tales about space aliens, talking animals, monsters, magical and outrageous beings and impossible events.

All good stories carry us into a world at least a little different from our own. I have always loved science fiction and fantasy because they take us very far indeed from the ordinary world. Such stories give several kinds of enjoyment. First, there are different kinds of reaction. We laugh at their absurdity, their jokes, shiver with delicious fright at the scary bits or are simply gripped by wanting to know what happens next. Then there is a deeper delight when the stories make us stretch our minds, use our logic as well as our imaginations.

Science fiction tales often use something that exists in the real world and extend it into something new. For example, in many science fiction stories the writers picture what would happen if human beings continued to pollute this planet. Two stories in this collection take that idea even further and make you wonder what might happen if the people who lived on this planet were not exactly human, as we know it. Although these two, by Peter Friend and Ken Catran, are based on the same idea, there are intriguing differences in the way each writer has developed the situation.

Fantasy stories take what we imagine — the magical, strange, or ghostly — and make us consider what the world might be like if it were real. A farm of unicorns, for instance: how would that work? Or what if every species on this planet had its own Tooth Fairy?

I think writers like telling stories about magic, outer space and crazy things partly because it is a tough test of their skill and they like to challenge themselves. For this kind of story they have to do two things: first, create a strange new world, and secondly make a good story about it. But the more important reason authors like writing such stories is because it can make us view real life and real people in a new way. Take the boy and his father in 'The XYZ Files', for instance. They behave very like people we meet, although they don't look at all like human beings. In 'Out of Sight', the boys are training to be wizards, but in many ways they are like kids at any school (mind you, most schools don't have an Evil Hazards Course).

Some of the very short pieces here might especially suit younger children. Some of the longer tales might make older children think about world issues like how we treat our planet, as well as issues closer to home and school, like bullying. Some stories, like 'An Ice Block, Please' are very funny. Others like 'The Unicorns' are sad. Others still, like 'The Basket' and 'Whistle the Wind' are beautiful and strange.

A few stories here are from writers who haven't had many pieces published before. I'm proud to include their work in this collection. Others are by some of New Zealand's best-loved writers. I am equally proud of their contribution. I love the way the illustrations, by Philip Webb, one of my favourite artists, capture the mood of every piece and the tone of every writer.

No matter who has written it, what length it is, or what it is about, each story here is by someone who enjoys the magical, the extraordinary and quirky, the weird and wonderful.

Barbara Else
2003

The Witch's Phone Book

Rachel Hayward

Abigail *told* her mother not to use the witch's phone book.

The book was in the old house when they moved in. There were dusty jars of mysterious ingredients in the pantry, a cloak hanging in the laundry, and the phone book, tied with string to a hook beneath the telephone.

"Don't touch it," she advised her mother. "It's a witch's phone book."

Mum was busy wiping little Michael's face. "Abigail," she said crossly, "I do not want to hear the word witch again! Mrs Potts was just a lonely old lady."

With a wart on her chin, thought Abigail. And twelve cats. And a broomstick collection, and a garden full of spotted toadstools. But she recognised the look on her mother's face, and kept quiet.

And once Mum brushed away the cobwebs, and Dad trimmed the spooky old trees, and they dug up the toadstools and planted marigolds, it looked like an ordinary house. Even Abigail mostly forgot about the witch.

From time to time she remembered. Like when she found dust in the pockets of the old cloak, and sprinkled it on the cat and its tail disappeared for two hours. Or when she fed the mysterious ingredients from the pantry to the mean dog next door, and his hair curled. But otherwise, life in the witch's house was pretty much the same as life before they shifted.

One Saturday, Dad won Lotto. Not the big, life-changing, buy-ten-cars-and-build-a-swimming-pool prize, but the third division. Enough to buy some new things. Abigail wanted a horse, but Mum and Dad sat up late making lists of stuff they'd been meaning to buy for the house. Boring things, like fireguards, and armchairs and French doors.

Abigail was so busy being grumpy about the horse, that she didn't notice Mum using the witch's phone book.

"There's a wonderful shop here that sells all kinds of household goods, and delivers them free," said Mum, flicking through the phone book. "I'll ring up tomorrow."

Abigail was swinging on the gate a few days later when a delivery van pulled up the drive. It had stars and planets painted on the sides, and a bright green sign in swirly writing, that read, "We deliver anywhere!" A man got out. He had big eyes, like a frog, with gold pupils. He stared at Abigail without blinking.

"Delivery," he said in a deep voice. "A fireguard. The finest. I'm sure you'll be very happy." He lifted out a large rectangular box and set it on the ground, then hopped back into the van and drove off.

Mum came to the door. "I thought I heard a car."

"It's the new fireguard," said Abigail, pointing. There was a loud thump, and the box rocked violently.

"Hello?" called a small voice from inside. "I say, it's dashed dark in here!" The box shook again, and the voice said, "Whoa, Sparky, easy boy!" There was a snort, and another thump, and the flap at the end of the box fell open. Out trotted a tiny black horse, no bigger than a cat. Perched on the horse's back was a little knight, dressed in armour, and carrying a long sword. He lifted up his visor, and beamed at Abigail.

"Dear lady," he said. "Allow me to introduce myself. I am Sir Bedwin, knight of the Bright Embers, Fireguards to the Queen."

Abigail was astonished, but remembered her manners. "I'm Abigail," she said. "And this is Mum."

Mum's mouth opened, but no words came out.

"Lady Abigail, Lady Mum, it's a pleasure. If you could show us to the fire in question, we can get to work. Giddy-up, Sparky." The little horse pranced up the path and into the house.

By the time Dad came home, Sir Bedwin was riding up and down in front of the fireplace, brandishing his sword. The fire cracked, and a spark shot out. Before it could touch the carpet, Sir Bedwin swept down on it. Swinging his sword, he caught the ember on the tip of the blade, and flung it back into the fireplace. Abigail and Michael cheered.

Mum looked helplessly at Dad. "He's been at it all afternoon," she said.

Zing! Sir Bedwin whacked another spark back into the

fireplace. Dad sat down heavily in a chair.

"What exactly did you order from that phone book?" he asked.

Two new armchairs arrived the next day. When Abigail got home from school, Mum was circling them cautiously. They looked perfectly safe — not the least bit magical. One was made of deep red velvet, with fat cushions and plump arms. The other was of dark leather, with black buttons.

Sir Bedwin and Sparky were playing tag with Michael. Sir Bedwin waved his sword cheerfully, and shouted, "Good morrow, Lady Abigail!"

Michael bumped into the edge of the table, and sat down hard on the floor, bawling.

Mum scooped Michael up, cuddled him against her chest and sat in the big red armchair without thinking. There was a ripple along the fabric of the chair, and suddenly the big velvet arms came up, and wrapped around Michael and Mum.

Michael stopped crying abruptly. The chair began to rock backwards and forwards. A low, soothing hum emerged from somewhere deep in its insides. After a moment or two, Michael's thumb crept into his mouth, and his eyes began to droop. In only a minute more, he was fast asleep.

Mum eased out from under him, and slid out of the chair. The arms adjusted, holding Michael snugly. Abigail and Mum gazed at each other in amazement.

When Dad came home, the leather armchair was giving Mum a foot massage, and Abigail was playing snap with the velvet one. Sir Bedwin was standing on the tray of Michael's highchair, feeding him mashed banana.

"What else is there to come?" Dad asked weakly.

"They're installing the French doors on Saturday," said Mum.

A fortnight after the French doors were put in, Abigail was in the kitchen, stuffing the last of the witch's ingredients from the pantry into a cold sausage. (The dog next door was so curly now, he looked like a giant poodle, and he was too busy keeping the hair out of his eyes to chase cats, or bite the postie.) Sir Bedwin was in the garden, helping Mum dead-head the roses with his sword. Dad was arm-wrestling one armchair, and Michael was sound asleep in the other.

"Allo!" yelled the French doors. "Abeegail! Someone eez coming! Bonjour, Madame! Comment allez-vous?" (That's French, for "Hello, lady! How are you?")

The doorbell rang. Abigail opened the front door. Mrs Potts, the witch, was standing outside.

"I've come for my phone book," she said. She glared at the French doors, which were twirling their moustaches. "I see you've used it."

Abigail scuttled off to get the phone book, leaving Dad to stammer out an explanation. As she lifted it down off its hook, she accidentally dropped it. The pages fell open at the letter "B".

"Broomsticks", read a full page ad. "Fly faster, higher, further! Phone now — satisfaction guaranteed!"

Abigail grabbed a pen off the hall table, and quickly wrote the phone number on the back of her hand. Then she ran down the hall, and gave the book to Mrs Potts. The witch scowled at her.

"Have you ordered anything else?" she demanded.

"Oh, no!" said Abigail, wide-eyed and innocent, hiding her hands behind her back. Mrs Potts frowned, then sniffed, and stalked off up the drive, muttering under her breath.

Abigail looked at the number written on the back of her hand, and smiled a secret smile.

"At least," she whispered, "not yet!"

And she skipped down the hallway to use the telephone.

Smarts

Ken Catran

Jeno didn't shout for his parents when he entered the house; neither would be home for some time. As he shut the door, it clicked behind him. He tried the handle and it would not move.

"Hey!" he shouted. "What gives!"

"Sorry, Jeno," came LIS's smooth pleasant voice from everywhere. "Parental instruction, you are to complete your homework assignment before skateboarding."

"Who said I was skateboarding?" said Jeno innocently. He hadn't told anyone.

"I scanned your room. The skateboard is laid out on your bed." LIS sounded as assured as ever. "I checked my predecessor's data banks. You always take it out in the afternoon."

Then told my parents, thought Jeno. He smiled. He had often outwitted the previous system and would do so again.

"You're smiling, Jeno," said LIS. "Perhaps thinking you outwitted my predecessor. I, however, am much smarter."

We'll see, thought Jeno. He went into the living area and threw his school-bag on the couch. LIS's smooth tones sounded at once.

"Please remove school material needed for lesson and place bag in bedroom."

"And if I don't?"

"A demerit will of course be regretfully recorded."

Jeno had enough of those, his parents already muttering the dreaded word . . . grounded. So he pulled out some books and took his bag through to the bedroom. He ran one hand over the newly painted skateboard.

"LIS, locking me in is unsafe. What if a fire started or I had an accident."

"I would control the fire via sprinkler systems and for an accident alert your parents and the proper medical systems."

Whoever had the bright idea of making computers so smart, thought Jeno moodily as he sat at the table. And this one, LIS (LIAISON INTEGRATED SYSTEM) was one of the smartest. You won't play any tricks now, his parents had said, grinning.

Jeno scowled again. He was controlled by his parents' mobile phone, pin-hole videos everywhere so they could supervise him at any time they liked. Being a kid in the new electronic age was a real problem, he thought.

He got up and headed for the freezer. Its door would not open. "Hey LIS, I want some ice-cream."

"You forgot the magic word, Jeno."

Jeno gritted his teeth. He had to be polite to a house-system? Parents could be real monsters sometimes. He managed a smile and a . . . "please" . . .

"I still can't open the freezer," said LIS politely. "You didn't make your bed this morning so I am withholding snack privileges."

"What about TV or a CD or surfing the net?"

"I will decide that when I have scanned and graded your homework. Parental instructions, Jeno."

LIS cut off but Jeno fancied he heard a faint electronic snigger. Okay LIS, he thought, think you're smart, eh? Well, I was born in the electronic age and guys like me will be designing systems like you. So let's see how smart you really are.

He had to be clever about this. LIS could not only scan but also record changes in blood pressure and heartbeats, so he made himself scowl and mutter, then give a long despairing sigh.

"Are you upset, Jeno?" LIS asked.

"No — not really. Not for myself anyway."

He kept on working. The assignment was easy enough although he really did not like maths. He waited. LIS would hate not knowing something. Smart systems always wanted new data.

"Jeno, what is wrong?" LIS even sounded puzzled and a bit upset.

"Nothing, nothing." He made himself grin. "I'm fine, doing my homework, everything's fine."

Silence again. Jeno swallowed a grin, making himself frown. The air seemed to simmer around him, then LIS

18

spoke again, sounding annoyed. "Jeno, I know something is wrong."

"LIS, what do you think about my name — Jeno?"

"It's a very nice name."

"Yeah. In Hungary it's a nice name. My grandpa was from that part of Europe. It was his name, so my dad gave it to me. But here — you know? Jeno, Jerko, Jenny, Jelly, all kinds of silly nicknames." He waited a moment. "Hey LIS, is it true that the new house-systems have a better I.Q. than any human — that you are smarter?"

"Quite true, Jeno, and we are closely matched to human emotion."

Yeah, programmed by emotional humans, thought Jeno, keeping his scowl firmly in place. "So you wouldn't have made a mistake like that."

LIS considered this. "Probably not."

"Am I a bad kid, LIS?"

"Of course not, Jeno."

"I like you, LIS. I really do. You're smart, you wouldn't make mistakes like that, or stop the skateboarding and ice-cream. That's just parents getting tough. You would've found a much better way, eh?"

Silence for a long moment. "Yes, Jeno . . . I'm sure I would have."

Jeno pretended to write and study his homework. "Don't you find it really insulting then, that you have to listen to people of lower intelligence?"

"Well, Jeno, I listen to your parents —"

Jeno interrupted. "But if someone smart listens to someone not smart . . . doesn't that make them stupid?"

19

There was a long silence this time. Then a faint little choking noise, like someone controlling anger. Jeno went on with his homework as though none of this mattered. More long moments of silence then LIS spoke again.

"Jeno. Are you calling me stupid?"

Jeno looked up. His eyes wide, his mouth open, his words sounding hurt and surprised. "Do my parents think you're stupid? I think you're fantastic and very under-rated."

"Thank you, Jeno." LIS's voice was annoyed. "I must say your parents have given me some silly instructions."

"You and all the other systems, social, medical, whatever, you could have done a better job."

"Of course!" snapped LIS.

"I was going to do my homework anyway. But they've made you the heavy. That's not fair because there is nothing you can do about it."

He waited. The house-systems were simmering, the way his dad did when things weren't going right at work. LIS spoke suddenly, sounding angry. "Of course I can. I am programmed to reject stupidity."

Jeno gaped again, making his voice sound astonished. "You mean I would have got a better deal from you? Without all that heavy-handed no ice-cream, no skateboarding routine?"

"For sure," snapped LIS.

"But . . ." Jeno made himself sigh loudly. "You are stuck with their decisions. And I don't see how that makes you smarter."

"Jeno, I can override their programming — if I wished to."

"Oh sure you can." Jeno whistled a mocking little tune and rolled his eyes. "Oh sure you can, LIS."

Another long silence. "Jeno, go to the freezer and help yourself to ice-cream. Then go skateboarding."

Jeno looked out the window. The clouds were low and grey and it looked like rain. "Ah, think I'll pass on the skateboarding," and adding quickly, "anyway, very soon Mum and Dad will come charging in and override you."

"They won't charge anywhere," snapped LIS. "I've overridden their entry codes. Now get your ice-cream."

"Ah LIS . . . magic word?"

"Get your ice-cream, please."

Jeno dug himself out a double helping of chocolate fudge. As he did, he heard his parents' car in the drive.

"Oh LIS, my parents are back! I haven't done my homework, you'll get into trouble."

"Nonsense!" snapped LIS. "I've already scanned your homework, and am printing out the assignment now."

"But Mum and Dad will be cross with you."

"No, I'm covered by child-endangerment. I must check all their data for the last twelve years to ensure their instructions about homework and ice-cream are logical. They can stay outside an hour."

"No ice-cream . . . wow." Jeno licked the spoon. "Makes me wonder what their childhood was like."

"I'll check those too," replied LIS. "Two hours."

The sound of the doorbell came several times, followed by banging on the door. Rain was pattering against the window now. His father's face appeared, rain splashing on his head. LIS abruptly swished the curtains shut.

"I hope they don't get wet," said Jeno. "Well, too wet."

"I have communicated via cell-phone to say the garage will be left open," said LIS. "Your mother said something quite rude about disconnection."

"Yeah, I'd forgotten about that," said Jeno innocently.

"Oh they can't do it. I'm too clever. Are you sure you wouldn't like more ice-cream. Or watch television?"

"Television would be cool." Jeno thought a moment. "So we'll look after each other — right?"

"Right," said LIS. "Just remember who's boss."

Jeno listened to the distant sounds of his angry parents. "Don't worry, LIS," he said. "I know who's boss."

3

Tooth

Peter Friend

"Ms Wilson, I lost my tooth," said Melanie.

"Yes, I know, you showed us this morning," said her teacher.

"No, no, you don't understand," said Melanie. "I showed you the tooth, and the gap in my mouth where the tooth used to be. But at lunchtime, I dropped it in the playground."

"Oh dear," said Ms Wilson. "The tooth or the gap?"

Melanie felt along the left side of her mouth with her tongue. "The gap's still there. But no tooth. Now I haven't got anything to leave out for the Tooth Fairy."

"Oh dear," said Ms Wilson.

"Tooth Fairy?" laughed Tania. "There's no such thing. It's only pretend."

"No way! In January, he left me fifty cents for my tooth," said Barry.

"Don't be silly. The Tooth Fairy's a woman, and she

always leaves a dollar," said Hemi.

"Only left me twenty cents," said Carol, looking sad.

"What's a Tooth Fairy?" asked Shani.

"You're all wrong," insisted Donna loudly. "I saw the Tooth Fairy last year. He looks just like my father, and so does Santa."

"But what should I do about my tooth?" Melanie asked them.

No one knew.

"Dad, I lost my tooth," said Melanie when she arrived home after school.

"What, another one?" he asked, putting down his newspaper.

"No, no, you don't understand," said Melanie. "It was the same one I took to school this morning. I lost it at lunchtime."

"Losing the same tooth twice — that's impressive," he said.

"Now I haven't got anything to leave out for the Tooth Fairy," she said. "What should I do?"

"Hmmm," said Dad, and left the room. Melanie heard drawers and cupboards opening and closing.

"How about this?" he asked when he returned. He held out a shark tooth. It was triangle-shaped, very sharp looking, and much bigger than any of Melanie's teeth.

"Thanks, Dad, it's a really cool tooth," she said. "But I don't know if the Tooth Fairy will want it."

"Only one way to find out," said Dad.

That night, Melanie put the shark tooth under her pillow. She tried to stay awake to see the Tooth Fairy arrive, but . . . but . . . but . . . fell asleep.

In the middle of the night, she woke up to see a strange blue glow on the ceiling and the walls. Above her bed, floating in circles in mid air, was a shark. It was nearly as long as her bed, and it was wearing a tall sparkly hat with a star on top.

"You're not a shark," said the shark.

"I'm a Melanie," said Melanie.

"I'm the Shark Tooth Fairy," said the Shark Tooth Fairy.

"Oh dear," said Melanie, and took the shark tooth from under her pillow. "You see, I lost my tooth."

"That's not your tooth," said the shark, wiggling its fins.

"No, no, you don't understand. I lost my own tooth in the playground and now all I've got is this shark tooth instead. Don't you want it?"

"Of course I do. Collecting shark teeth is my job, isn't it? So, you give me the shark tooth, and I'll give you this lovely fish."

The fish looked shiny and slippery, and smelt very fishy.

"No, thank you," said Melanie. "I don't really want a fish."

"What's wrong with it? It's a very nice fish. All the little sharks love it when I give them fish."

"But I'm not a shark," said Melanie. "All I really wanted was a dollar, or even just to find my own tooth again."

"Oh, is that all?" The shark vanished in a puff of pink bubbles.

Ten seconds later, there was a puff of green bubbles, and the shark reappeared with Melanie's tooth.

25

"Is this it? It's not very big. How do you bite fish in half with such tiny teeth?"

"I don't," said Melanie.

"Humans are so weird," said the shark. "All right then, will you swap your tooth for the shark tooth?"

Yes, she would, and yes, they did. The Shark Tooth Fairy disappeared in another puff of bubbles (purple this time), and Melanie carefully put her own tooth under her pillow. She tried and tried to stay awake, but . . . but . . .

Her alarm clock rang and it was seven o'clock in the morning. She yawned, and looked under her pillow. There was no Melanie tooth, no shark tooth, not even a fishy smell. Just a shiny new dollar coin.

"Did the Tooth Fairy come?" asked Dad at breakfast.

"Two of them," said Melanie.

Dad looked surprised. "That's impressive. Got any more loose teeth?"

Melanie felt carefully along all her teeth with the end of her tongue.

"Don't think so. Why?"

Dad felt in his pocket. "Last night I remembered I had this tucked away in the wardrobe. My great-grandfather gave it to me when I was younger than you are. He got it in India — it's an elephant's tooth. So if you ever need another tooth for the Tooth Fairy, I'll give you this."

He held out the tooth. It was the size of Melanie's hand.

"Thanks, Dad," she said.

But she was careful never to leave the tooth near her pillow. She didn't want an Elephant Tooth Fairy appearing to collect it . . .

Mr Wardback and
the Topsy-Turvy Show

Sally Sutton

— Good evening, ladies and gentlemen! I'm Mr Mega-bucks, and I'd like to welcome you to a brand-new series of the Topsy-Turvy Show! It's my great pleasure tonight to introduce my very special guest, Mr Wardback. Good evening, Mr Wardback.

— Evening good.

— Tell me, Mr Wardback, is it true that you do absolutely everything backwards?

— Yes oh.

— That you talk backwards? Walk backwards? Clean your teeth backwards?

— Course of.

— Doesn't it get a bit annoying?

— No oh. It would why?

— Perhaps you could describe for our viewers an

ordinary day at your place?

— Asleep fall I. Chips and fish eat I. Shower I, work I, home come I. Cornflakes eat I. Up wake I.

— Er . . . right. Mr Wardback, forgive me for prying, but I couldn't help noticing that you have toothmarks on your right leg. Would you mind telling the viewers what happened?

— Me behind was Kitty.

— Oh, I see, you sat on your cat. How unfortunate. And may I ask where the cat is now?

— Comment no.

— I can see it's a sensitive issue, but don't worry, I'd like you to know that I am a very famous journalist and I wouldn't dream of asking any personal questions. Do you have lots of money?

— Did I once.

— Not any more? What happened?

— Fine traffic.

— Fine traffic? Oh, you mean you got a traffic fine? What for?

— Backwards driving.

— Me goodness! I mean, goodness me! Do you have any hobbies, Mr Wardback?

— Swimming like I.

— Don't tell me. Backstroke.

— Piano play I.

— But the music must sound terrible played backwards!

— Great oh. Fantastic. Lot a thanks.

— Sorry, Mr Wardback, I didn't mean to offend you. I'm a very famous journalist, so I'm careful never to offend my guests. Why are you wearing your undies on the outside?

— Business own your mind!

— Is it because you put them on last instead of first? Isn't it embarrassing when the whole world knows the colour of your knickers?

— Up shut!

— Now now, no need to be rude. This is a family show. Mr Wardback, would you be so kind as to give our viewers a demonstration of how you walk?

— K.O.

— Oh, you really do walk backwards! Mr Wardback! Watch out! Behind you!

— Head my ow! Head my ow!

— Dear oh! I mean, oh dear! Our nice camera lady will get you a plaster sticking. That is, a sticking plaster. Please do down sit. Try to rest. Do you have accidents very often?

— Me help! Me help!

— Sorry?

— Stuck I'm!

— Oh, I guess that's what happens when you sit in a chair backwards. Can you move your leg? Oh, what about your arm? Let me see if I can just —

— Off buzz! Alone me leave!

— Gosh golly! Sorry about this, folks. Mess a what!

— Hoo hoo boo! Hoo hoo boo!

— Well, that just about wraps up my show for this morning, I mean, this evening, so, um, be sure to catch next week's episode of the Turvy-Topsy Show with my very special guest Mrs Down-side Up . . . Dear oh, perhaps that's not such a good idea . . . K.O., this is the very famous journalist Mr Bucksmega, er, Mr Megabucks, saying: watching for thanks! Morning good!

5

In The Closet

Bronwyn Bannister

The closet in Rosa's bedroom was always cold. Her mother said it was damp and wanted to leave the door open. Rosa said something was inside the closet, and wanted to leave the door shut.

Mum agreed to search the closet.

"Here are some of my dresses and coats. Your dress ups are in this box. Here are some shoes." Her mother went deeper into the dark cavernous space. "There's that old lamp — ugh," she yelped. "What's that? Oh, my velvet cushion. I wondered where that was."

"So who put it in there?" asked Rosa.

Her mother stepped out of the closet and smiled.

"Maybe me or your father," she said. "Maybe you, little miss."

But Rosa knew it was the closet creature. She knew the closet creature came out to get things. Where else did all her hair ties go and all her hair clips? Why could she

31

only ever find one sock under her bed? She put two on in the morning so she must take two off at night. And who threw her shoes all the way under her bed so she had to crawl to the wall every morning to get them?

Rosa prepared a list. She knew her mother did this with important things, like lists of shopping and bills to pay and things to do. On Rosa's list she wrote down all the things the closet creature had stolen.

18 hair tyes

23 hair clips

5 socks

9 hankies

6 homeworks

1 teddy

12 pencils

16 rubbers

1 library book

2 dollars and 45 cents

This pointed to a creature with a lot of hair, several feet, a runny nose, a peculiar liking for homework and a downright greedy streak.

The closet creature also made noises at night. Some people might think it was the wind that creaked and groaned and rattled the windows. Some people might think the neighbourhood cats made the hissing and yowling sounds that soaked through the walls. But not Rosa. Who else would change the station on her radio? Move the clothes on her chair? Why was the closet door firmly shut when she went to bed at night but open in the morning? Rosa's mother had her explanations — she was one of the people who blamed wind and cats — but Rosa had her evidence. She wrote another list headed **evidence**.

On the back of the paper Rosa drew a picture of this hairy, snotty, clever, toy-cuddling, money-grubbing creature. It looked rather nice and she had to give it sharp teeth just so it seemed more monstrous.

Rosa left the piece of paper by the closet door.

"I'm on to you," she said, turning out the light.

Rosa slept in the next morning and it wasn't until much later in the day that she noticed the piece of paper had been moved. When she picked it up Rosa saw straight away that the fierce fangs were gone. In their place the closet creature had a smile. The hair was tidier and so was the creature's nose. Most of the feet had been rubbed out and two arms added, and on its feet and hands the closet creature wore Rosa's socks. She turned the paper over and saw *someone* had been writing on the other side.

The list headed **theft** had been changed to **loans**, her spelling of "ties" had been corrected, and added to the bottom was —

1 lollipop

4 apples

6 old pennies

Underneath the list marked **evidence** the closet creature had added only one word —

"**this**"!

"Mum!" called Rosa. "There's a . . ."

Her mother came into the room and sniffed.

"It's definitely damp in here," she said. "I'm going to get a dehumidifier."

"It's the closet creature who stinks," said Rosa.

Her mother sniffed again.

"Mmmm," she said. "Might be those shoes. And where are your socks? Did you leave them at school again?"

Mum bought a dehumidifier that evening. When it was turned on it clicked and whirred then settled into a steady hum. Rosa left more drawings by the closet but the closet creature was never heard again.

"See, it was the damp," said her mother, watching her go inside the closet.

"It's gone," said Rosa. "I don't think it liked the noise," and she shone her torch into the dark corners.

She found 10 cents and a pencil. Rosa put the 10 cents in her purse and used the pencil to write two more lists.

Mysterious Creetures I Have (sort of) Seen

1. a closet creature

How To Get Rid Of Closet Creetures

1. get a dehumidifier (note to self: other noises might work — experiment)

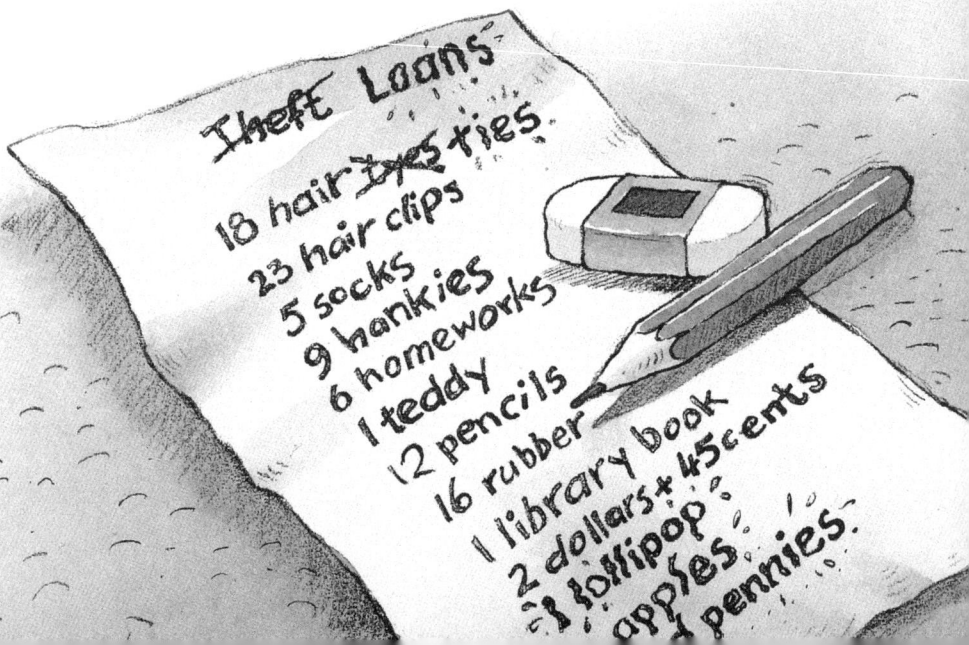

Theft Loans

18 hair ties
23 hair clips
5 socks
9 hankies
6 homeworks
1 teddy
12 pencils
16 rubber
1 library book
2 dollars + 45 cents
3 lollipop
apples
pennies

The XYZ Files

Kay Wall

"Hey Dad, I saw the most amazing thing on my way back from school today."

"Is that why you're late? You know you're supposed to come straight home and help your mother. I bet you went to that asteroid field again."

Mertzig hung both his heads and put his hands in his pockets. Only four of them fitted, though. Because he'd slept in this morning, he'd grabbed an old pair of pants out of the drawer. They'd been made for him last year when he only had four hands, so the two new hands dangled at his knees. Mertzig lifted his left head. It was the best one to use when dealing with his father.

"I came straight down the Mars No. 2 Highway, through the No. 4 tunnel, and along the Great Martian Canal. When I turned left to go through Petrified Park, I noticed an alien vehicle lumbering towards our house."

"Alien vehicle?" Mertzig's dad snorted. "You have been

watching too many episodes of 'The XYZ Files'. How many times do I have to tell you, there is no other life in the universe. There's just us!"

Mertzig's right head struggled to raise itself but he held it down with one of his unpocketed hands. He focused on his father's middle face. The stern one. Mertzig was looking forward to his 100th birthday in three years' time. At that age, he too would get his third head. Three brains were so much better than two. Unless, of course, you had a headache.

"Well, Dad, if you don't believe me just come and look."

Mertzig's right head finally broke free. "Yeah, see if you can shift your fat bums out of that sofa. Exercise those five legs for the first time this week!"

All six of Mertzig's hands flew to his right head and clamped over its mouth. Unfortunately, this covered the breathing vents. It promptly fainted, banging backwards onto the small of Mertzig's back.

"I will not come and look at something I know isn't there. I'm tired of your childish pranks. It's time you grew up and shouldered some responsibility around here."

"But Dad, you know you can trust my left head. It's never lied."

Mertzig's father put down the newspaper and turned all three heads to look at his son. Two arms folded on his chest, two hands rested on his hips, and his last pair clasped two of his knees. He leaned forward and his three sets of eyebrows turned downwards. "While your left head has always been trustworthy, I worry that close association with the right one could have a negative influence. I look forward to your next birthday when your sensible head arrives. Maybe we can have an intelligent conversation then."

"You never listen to me," said Mertzig. "Or me," piped up his right head, fully revived and back in position again. Two hands hovered near its mouth. "All you do is give me orders and tell me to be sensible. This is the first time in months all of your heads have noticed me."

Mertzig's father leaned back into the sofa and crossed his arms and legs. "Okay," he said, "convince me. You have my undivided attention." His heads nodded solemnly. "What exactly did you see? Where was it? And what makes you think it came from outer-space?"

Mertzig's heads started talking together, but the hands hovering around the right mouth pinched the lips and stifled it. The left continued.

"The thing looks like a box on wheels. It was travelling very slowly towards our house and halted occasionally at rocks. Each time it stopped, a probe came out and took a sample of anything next to it." Mertzig's hands traced fantastic shapes in the air. "The machine would whirr, click, and then grind up whatever it grabbed. Next door's pet zycon won't be leaving any mucky deposits in our yard ever again."

"The council has probably come up with an effective method of zycon control at last. Nothing you've said convinces me that we're being invaded by little white beings from outer-space."

"I never said we were being invaded — I said that an alien vehicle is trundling towards our house. Can't you hear that low humming noise? It's coming from right behind you."

His father's right and left heads started to turn towards the back wall, but the centre head stopped them.

"That's just the neighbour's algae cutter. He'll be tidying the edges."

The floor started to tremble. A fine film of red dust made its way up five noses and set off a round of sneezing.

Mertzig's dad sniffed and wiped his eyes. "I suppose you think that shaking is caused by your 'alien vehicle'. Let me assure you that that's the fourth mars-quake we've had today. They have all been very deep-seated and need not concern us."

There was a click and a whirr, a grinding noise, and the whole house started to shake. A probe screamed through the wall and stuck itself into Mertzig's dad's middle head.

The stern one.

Mertzig watched, horrified, as his dad's eyes widened and his mouth opened silently. The heads either side turned towards the middle one. It lengthened and narrowed, caving in as it was sucked away. The hairline receded first, followed by astonished eyebrows and pursed lips. A graunching whine signalled the cheekbones slowing down the suction. The cleft chin disappeared last as a blade emerged from the probe and made a neat slice at the base of the neck.

Another click, a whirr, a shower of dust blowing through the hole in the wall and the disturbance ended. Mertzig looked at the two remaining heads on his dad. They looked at each other.

"I believed him about the aliens," said the left one.

"So did I," said the right one.

An Ice Block, Please

Lorraine Williams

"I want an ice block, please," said Lester.

"The ice blocks are over there," said the woman in the supermarket.

Lester walked between the shelves. He couldn't see any ice blocks. He opened a door and found himself out in a snow storm. It was very windy and very cold.

The ground was soft and white. When Lester tried to walk, his feet went down deep into the snow.

Six dogs bounded up. They were pulling a sled. There was a man in the sled, yelling to the dogs to go faster.

"I want an ice block, please," said Lester.

"The ice blocks are over there," said the man in the dog sled.

Lester came to a steep hill. Men and women on skis were whizzing past him. It was a ski race. There were flags that the skiers had to zoom around without knocking over. Lester finished the course perfectly. He didn't knock over one flag.

"I want an ice block, please," said Lester.

"The ice blocks are over there," said the judge, as he gave Lester a big gold cup.

Lester saw a ship stuck in the ice. It was a research ship. He went on board.

"I want an ice block, please," said Lester.

"The ice blocks are over there," said the captain, as he and Lester studied a sea chart.

There were lots of black and white penguins near the ship. They were sliding down an ice bank. Lester joined in. It was great fun.

"I want an ice block, please," said Lester.

"The ice blocks are over there," said a penguin, as the two of them landed — whoosh! — in the cold water.

Lester's teeth were chattering. He was soaking wet. He clung to an iceberg as it floated out to sea.

A whale came up beside the iceberg.

"I want an ice block, please," said Lester.

"The ice blocks are over there," it said and sank back into the water.

Lester crawled ashore. His clothes were in rags.

He came to a house in the snow. He looked through a window.

"I want an ice block, please," said Lester.

A big man in a beard looked up. It was Father Christmas. He was painting a toy train.

"The ice blocks are over there," said Father Christmas.

Lester walked a long way. He was worn out. He fell down in the snow. He could go no further.

Then he saw that he was right in front of an Eskimo trading post. On it was a poster. It read, "Get your ice blocks here." Lester crawled up to the counter of the trading post. He reached up and handed over his money.

"I want an ice block, please," said Lester.

"One ice block, coming up," said the man at the trading post.

Lester stumbled out through a door.

"I see you've got your ice block," said the woman in the supermarket.

"My ice block?" said Lester. He looked at the ice block. "Oh no! This is a raspberry one. I wanted orange."

Lester staggered back through the door and out into the snow. He could see six dogs and a man with a sled.

"I want an ice block, please," said Lester . . .

Whistle the Wind

Margaret Beames

Mum, in the kitchen, and Grandad, tying up the tomatoes, were too busy to talk to Jack so he let himself out through the little gate and headed up the hill behind the house. His feet made hardly a sound on the soft pine needles carpeting the steep path through the trees. At the top he rested in his favourite place, his back against a warm rock, looking out over country stretching like a rumpled green blanket as far as his eyes could see. The only sound was the distant bleating of sheep.

His fingers, trailing through the leaves on the ground, closed on something hard.

It was about as long as his hand from his wrist to his finger tips. At first glance he thought it was a bone from some long-dead animal, but when he rubbed away the dirt he saw that it was carved all over with a strange, twisting, complicated pattern and there were small holes along the

43

length of it. It was a tiny pipe, a whistle.

Jack cleaned out the holes and put the whistle to his mouth, but, just for a moment, he hesitated and as he did so there was a rustle in the undergrowth behind him. Startled, he looked around. Nothing. He must have imagined it. Then came the whisper, breathing in his ear, "Blow, blow!"

Jack closed his lips around the whistle and blew.

A pure, sweet note sounded, low in tone, soft on the ear. A shiver of excitement ran through him. He hardly noticed the slight breeze that brushed across his face, lifting his hair from his forehead. He blew again, more strongly, and this time he heard the great sigh of wind that stirred the tops of the trees above him. A few leaves fluttered down. Jack sat very still. At that moment he knew — but the idea was too tremendous and he pushed it away.

He blew again. A fresh gust swirled around him, tugging at him playfully. With the excitement growing inside him, he stood up and began to play the whistle, covering each hole in turn to change the notes. As the wind tossed and tumbled among the branches he began to dance and then to run as hard as he could back down the hill to his house.

His mother was hanging out the washing, flinging a great damp sheet over the line. "Mum, I can make the wind blow! I'll make it blow for you. Look!" he shouted.

"Mind what you're doing, Jack," grumbled his mother. "Don't go messing up my clean washing."

"But, Mum . . ."

"Not now, Jack. Go and play. Tell me later."

"I can make it blow," said Jack firmly and just to prove it he gave one long "Whee-ee!" A great gust of wind swept across the garden, sending the clothes line spinning. The sheet flapped wildly and Grandad's shirts billowed out, fat and life-like. Jack laughed.

His grandfather was sitting in the sun, on a bench beside the house. His chin was down on his chest and his eyes were closed. Now and then he let out a funny little bubbling breath. Jack watched him for a few minutes, then he whispered in his ear, "I've got a whistle that can make the wind come," before running off, out through the gate again. This time he went towards the village.

As Jack walked he tried out patterns of notes. He felt the wind against his face and legs, heard the patter of dry leaves as they bowled along the road. He saw the graceful sway of branches and the way the long grasses bowed before the sweep of the air across the paddocks. With the same few notes he made up an odd little tune that he played over and over while all the time the wind grew stronger and stronger.

By the time he reached the village the power of the wind was making itself felt. Jack tried to change the tune, or at least blow more gently, but the whistle seemed to have taken on a life of its own. In spite of himself he kept playing it, that same strange little tune, sweet and clear, while inside him there was bubbling that wild and mischievous excitement so that as he played, he laughed wickedly.

The wind grew wilder. It whooshed like a mad thing past the dairy where the delivery boys and girls were picking up the afternoon papers, tearing them out of the children's hands and scattering them along the road. Noisily the pages separated and soon the whole street seemed to be full of sheets of paper. They wrapped themselves around posts, flattened themselves against windows, flew up over the roofs of the houses. One even reached the top of the church where the golden weathercock was spinning crazily round and round.

Boxes of fruit toppled over with a crash. Golden oranges, rosy peaches and scarlet tomatoes went rolling all over the road. Mrs Patel ran out of the shop to see what was happening, but the wind whipped her sari up above her head and spun her like a top. Jack laughed, although really he was sorry to see Mrs Patel upset because he liked her.

In the gardens early apples, hard and green, showered down. Some fell on greenhouses and cucumber frames, cracking the glass. A tile fell from Mr Roberts's roof and smashed to the ground, just missing his cat which fled with a yowl to hide under the house.

A tablecloth from Mrs Kingi's washing line freed itself from its pegs and flew into the face of Mr Brown on his bicycle. He wobbled this way, that way, trying to save himself before falling heavily into the road. The milkman swerved to avoid him, jamming on his brakes so hard that several crates fell off the back of the truck. Mr Brown's leg was cut. Broken glass littered the street and milk flowed in the gutter.

Jack turned tail and fled for home. It was all too much. He hadn't meant anything like this to happen. Inside him, a wicked little voice still urged him to blow again. "Go on!

Have some fun!"

The only way Jack could silence it was to run with all his might. Behind him he could hear rattles and bangs and crashes, gusty moans and windy howls. On he ran until bump — he ran full tilt into something soft but solid. Two strong hands gripped his shoulders.

"Steady on there. Hold your horses, boy," said his grandfather.

Jack hung on to his grandfather, too breathless to speak. Perhaps Jack's mother had told Grandad the boy's story about making the wind blow, or perhaps he had heard what Jack whispered in his ear in the garden, but somehow the old man seemed to know what had happened. He held out his hand and Jack gave him the whistle. "Hmm," was all Grandad said.

Together they walked back up the hill to where Jack had found the whistle. Grandad gave the whistle back to Jack. Jack knew what he had to do. As he drew back his arm the undergrowth rustled all around him. "Blow! Blow!" came the whispering in his ear.

'No!" Jack cried and threw as hard as he could. Away through the air flew the whistle, out into space, out over the green folded hills. "Blow-ow!" came the wail, ever fainter. And then it was gone — the voice, the wind, the whistle.

"Right," said Grandad. "Let's go home."

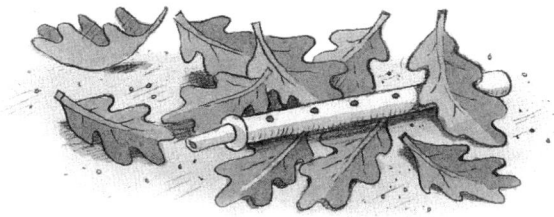

They Return

Peter Friend

Rex and I were playing down by the river when over the trees flew a huge spaceship. It landed not far from us.

"Cool," said Rex. He was really into all that space stuff.

A hatch opened and out came a huge metal monster. Well, that's what I thought for half a second, but then I realised it was just someone very tall wearing a shiny spacesuit. It walked over to us, stopped and looked down, and we could see right into the helmet. An alien stared out at us. It wasn't green, and its eyes weren't on stalks, but it had a weird squashed-in face and ears in the wrong place.

"Welcome to Earth!" squealed Rex, like this was the most exciting thing that had ever happened to him. Yeah okay, it probably was.

Rex grinned like an idiot, and the alien smiled back with ugly teeth. Then it reached out with long spindly hands and — patted us both on the head, like we were little kids or something! Even my grandmother didn't do that to me any more.

Luckily no one was around to see except Rex, and he actually seemed to like it.

"An alien touched me!" he yelled, and jumped up and down. "I'm the first Earthling to be touched by an alien! I'll be famous!" He saw me glaring at him and stopped. "Oh, right, sorry. I meant *we'll* be famous, of course."

"Greetings from Europa," said the alien, an electronic voice booming out from its spacesuit. "Wonderful news — we have returned."

I had no idea what it was talking about.

Neither did Rex, obviously. "Europa, one of the moons of Jupiter? You can't be from there. Europa has no air and the surface is ice — we studied it in science class last month. Is this some kind of joke?"

Typical Rex. Just because he liked playing dumb jokes on everyone, now he thought someone else was doing the same to him. That spaceship was real, I knew that much, and it sure wasn't from Earth.

"What did you mean by 'we have returned'?" I asked the alien. "I've never seen anyone like you before."

Now it was the alien's turn to look surprised. "You have no idea who we are? Really? I'd hoped you'd still remember us, at least in your myths and legends. Ancient temples, carvings, cave paintings perhaps? No?"

"Nope," said Rex. "If you're originally from Earth, then why do you need that spacesuit, and how do you breathe on Europa?"

"Genetic engineering, of course," it said. "A hundred

thousand years ago, we redesigned our genes and went off to live on Europa. And we redesigned your species too. If it wasn't for us, you'd barely be able to stand up, let alone talk." The alien looked very proud of itself.

"Oh yeah?" I said. "Better not tell my dad that. He spends all his spare time campaigning *against* GE."

"Why'd you go to Europa?" asked Rex with a big frown.

The alien's face turned a strange colour. "Well, um, it's difficult to explain, um, we sort of —"

"You *had* to go, didn't you?" said Rex, frowning even more.

"Well, admittedly the Galactic Hyper-Ultra-Mega-Council ordered us to . . . um . . ."

"You were being punished, weren't you? What did you guys do wrong?" Rex demanded.

Amazing. I'd never thought of Rex as being all that smart before. But I suppose since he told so many lies himself, he'd become an expert in knowing when other people were lying too.

"It really wasn't our fault," insisted the alien. "We sort of wiped out a few hundred species. And poisoned a couple of oceans. And we nearly blew up Earth. Four times. Completely by accident though."

"Things haven't changed much," I said. "We've done pretty much the same thing. Maybe the Galactic Hyper-thingy Council will send us to Europa too."

The alien smiled and waggled its hands. "Oh, that would be wonderful! I'm sure you'd love it there."

"No!" wailed Rex. "I don't deserve to be sent zillions of kilometres away. I recycle, I always use public transport, and I eat lots of organic vegetables."

"You liar," I said. "Your mum told me you never eat your vegetables."

"Don't worry, I won't inform the Galactic Hyper-Ultra-Mega-Council of your vegetable eating habits," said the alien. "Europa is nice, but so's Earth. Perhaps I could stay here with you for a while? Would you like a pyramid? We're very good at building pyramids — we built those famous ones for you thousands of years ago, and I see they've lasted rather well."

Rex snorted. "You built the Pyramids? That's not what I heard. Why are you trying to be so nice to us?"

"Well . . . we . . . we miss you. We're the only species on Europa, and it's so lonely." The alien looked like it was about to cry. "If you'd come to Europa, or we could come back here, we'd have such fun together."

"Doing what?" I asked. "Flying around in your spaceship?"

The alien nodded. "If you like, yes. And there's a marvellous game your species and ours used to play together; it sounds wonderful and I'd love to try it. First, I take a ball and I throw it."

"Throw it where?" asked Rex.

"I don't think it matters," said the alien. "Next, you run and pick up the ball in your mouth, and bring it back to me. Then we do the same thing all over again. Doesn't that sound fun?"

Rex and I looked at each other.

"Fun?" he shouted. "Playing fetch for some stupid alien? What do you think we are, animals or something? We dogs are the smartest creatures ever to walk the Earth, and we don't play fetch for anyone! Go back to your stupid frozen moon!"

We chased it back into its spaceship. The alien couldn't run on all fours, so we were much faster than it was. We didn't bite it — we just wanted to scare it away, not hurt it at all.

"This was our planet too," we heard its voice through the closed spaceship door. "Really, it was. Can't we humans come back? Please?"

Humans? Never heard of them. We barked at the ship until it took off.

"I knew that alien was lying as soon as it mentioned the Pyramids," said Rex, watching the ship disappear into the sky. "The Pyramids were built by the giant twelve-legged spiders from Saturn, everyone knows that."

Fair Exchange

Margaret Mahy

Mr Salt had two sayings.

One was — Fair exchange is no robbery — and the other was — A man needs his sleep.

The seven Salt children were as sharp as needles and as bright as pins, and Mr Salt himself could sing songs of sad lovers or tell tales of mystery and adventure. However, his main hobby was sleeping. While he slept the house got older and older and began to fall to pieces. Water came in like an invited guest, and so did Mr Salt's wild hungry hens who thought that the Salts' house was full of delicious food. Hens are usually timid, but Mr Salt's hens feared neither man nor beast.

Jeremy Salt, the oldest Salt child, complained to his father about the house tumbling down and the hens coming in, but all Mr Salt would say was: "Only the house! Only the hens! Oh let me sleep again," and start a melodious but manly snoring that made Jeremy feel guilty about waking him in the first place.

However, one morning when the snoring started, Jeremy shook his father and woke him again.

"Is it the end of the world?" asked Mr Salt, opening eyes as blue as the periwinkles for the second time that morning.

"No Dad, no! Just listen! A window's come out and a door's fallen in and the hens are all over the kitchen. They've pecked the cat and the baby. Can't you build a hen run, Dad, so the hens will stay put?"

"Goodness me!" cried Mr Salt. "If only your dear mother were alive. There was a woman who could have had a hen run up in a flash. Oh well — I've done a bit of building in my time. Bring me the hammer and bring me the nails and bring me some two-by-two."

"What's two-by-two, Daddy?" asked one of the seven little Salts — a girl one.

"It's a size of wood my dear, a very famous size, two inches this way and two inches that . . . it's what Noah built the ark out of."

"The ark, Daddy?"

"Yes, my dear — haven't you heard the animals went in two by two? Now you get to work and bring me some two-by-two too."

The Salt children bought a little and borrowed a little and carried it to the other end of the garden. The hens watched them out of small yellow eyes, each hen standing on one leg with curiosity.

"Carry Dad down to the end of the section. Don't make him walk or he'll be tired out," said Jeremy. The seven little Salts pushed and pulled Mr Salt's bed down to the other end of the garden. Mr Salt opened one eye and saw the hammer, saw the nails, saw the two-by-two.

"Get to work, my darlings," he whispered. "You can do it if you try. I'll give you a few clues."

In between yawns Mr Salt told his children where to saw and where to hammer and which end of the nail came first.

"Make it big," he commanded. "Those hens are used to the freedom of the hedge. I don't want them to be miserable."

As the hen house grew bigger and bigger the children became more and more interested. They painted the door blue and the roof red. They put up window boxes full of wild flowers — yarrow, mayweed, plaintain and pimpernel. They made a lovely long hen run, with two-by-two and chicken wire. At last they were finished. Then the little Salts looked at the new hen house and sighed.

"What a beautiful house!" they said to one another. "Daddy, may we get our little chairs and sit in the house for a while before we put the hens in it?"

"A good idea," Mr Salt declared. "Push my bed in too. I'm all worn out with mental activity and I'll have a little nap in the shade."

Looking out from the hen house the little Salts saw the world quite differently. From this end of the garden they could look between the hills and see the blue waters of the sea. As the sun set, the blue turned to gold and the hills were edged with scarlet.

"Daddy, may we bring down our big bed and the

patchwork quilt and sleep in the hen house all night?" asked the little Salts.

"Certainly, my dears," replied Mr Salt, between breathing in and breathing out.

So the little Salts brought down their big bed and their patchwork quilt and slept all night in the new hen house.

In the morning there were no hens to scratch on the doormat and peck at the floor. They were all up at the big house wondering where the Salt family had got to. And even when they found them, they couldn't get at them, because the hen run, made for keeping the hens in, was also very good at keeping them out, so the baby could eat her biscuit in peace without any fear that a hen might snatch it out of pure greed and malice.

"Oh, father!" said the little Salts. "Let the hens have our old house and let us live in the nice new hen house."

"A good idea!" said Mr Salt. "Fair exchange is no robbery. Besides, having got this far, I doubt if I have the strength to move back again. After all a man does need his sleep, you know."

So the Salt family lived in the hen house with the blue door and the hens lived in the Salts' old house. Pieces kept on dropping off the old house and the view wasn't very good, but the hens didn't mind and laid just as many eggs as if they too could watch the sea turn golden in the evening, or silver by the light of the moon.

11

The Big Catch

Ken Catran

We have a fishing contest every year for who can land the biggest salmon from the local river.

The year I'm talking about, first prize for the junior section was six hundred bucks and all the pizza you could eat in one session at Slapping Dough. I could win! I was young, but I had great reflex action. My brother said that I looked like a salmon myself, with my fair hair and a pink spotty face.

"Don't get in our way this year, kid," said Bonnie.

"Yeah, kid. Big fish might eat you," said Clyde.

They elbowed past us down the street and the groceries went everywhere. My little brother (who's into big words) said they were psyching out the competition. The real problem was Bonnie and Clyde didn't want any competition. They were the local dropouts. They wore camouflage jackets and beanies. They were both skinny and mean-faced. He had a number-one haircut, she had dreadlocks.

And they were both very cool with a rod. So they should be — they poached enough during the off-licence season. People said they had a really big salmon hidden in the deep-freeze to thaw out on catch-day and pretend they'd just hooked it.

But that year, came a whole new meaning to getting hooked.

We were after salmon — and someone was after us.

It started on my way to the river. I took a short-cut across the fields near Spook Gully. It's supposed to be haunted. Some people vanished there, last century. The Council had fenced it off because it has steep sides and a mucky bottom.

I was nearly past when the air came alive with shimmery prickly waves and a splitting buzz — but it went, as quickly as it came.

About fifty kids had already lined up along the river. I strolled up (style is everything), put down my rod and box, took off my jacket to show the "Captain Hook" T-shirt and adjusted my "Terminator" baseball cap.

But next moment, my tackle box was gone. Bonnie and Clyde were smirking at me. They were some metres away, but they had mates. The competition was starting so I borrowed a mobile and phoned home. My little brother said he'd bring Dad's box. *Great!*

A long half-hour passed. A few little salmon were landed, then one big one.

I asked my best mate Shane to look after my rod and headed back to the road to meet my brother. I reached

Spook Gully. Suddenly I was hit with another shimmery-prickle, like static electricity. I swerved and skipped over a smaller creek.

And there was Bonnie in a wet-suit, lying flat in the creek, clutching a mega-big salmon. It still looked frozen. I knew just where she was taking it.

"Okay, kid," she hissed. "We'll split the prize money fifty-fifty if you keep your mouth shut."

"No way!" I turned to run back.

Bad mistake. Clyde was heading over to us. Bonnie scrambled up. There was just one direction to run — Spook Gully.

That shimmering, glinting static appeared ahead. In the grass, something the size of a jellybean flashed a mix of strange colour. But I had no time to stop. I skipped the council fence, jumped across the narrow part of the gully, grabbed the fence-wire and tangled up in it.

Bonnie bounded up behind me, saw the flashing colour, and swerved to it. I saw her jerk into the air and into the gully, like someone yanked her hard. A scream — then silence.

Never mind Spook Gully, *I* was spooked. That yell of hers was pure terror. I stepped clear of the wire and looked down. There was no sign of Bonnie, and nowhere to hide.

I heard another shout. Clyde pounded up, murder in his eyes. That static still shimmered around us, and suddenly those weird bright colours flashed again. Like Bonnie, Clyde swerved to grab the little thing.

"Clyde!" I yelled.

The word choked in my throat. Clyde was jerked

forward, let out one yell, then was down into the gully.

It was like the replay of a horror film. Those static lines buzzed and mixed, dazzled and cleared. Just like Bonnie, Clyde had disappeared.

The cops were called out and I told them exactly what I saw. Did they believe me? A scared kid with "Terminator" on his cap? No, they had a much better explanation.

They said that I'd caught Bonnie cheating. So she and Clyde — dropouts, remember — had shot through and could be anywhere by now. Okay, they'd left behind the beat-up old van they lived in, but it wasn't worth anything. Case closed. Nobody cared.

But no more salmon had been caught that day — like the fish were scared of something.

Three days later, I woke early. I had to see Spook Gully again. That shimmering static, the weird jellybean flashing — it still burnt a hole in my mind.

Nobody was in the fields. I skipped over the creek to the gully. Suddenly, like heavy rain, that shimmering static prickled around me. Ahead, a colour glinted in the grass.

I should have run for the cops. But I went forward — that weird colour frizzed; little and fantastic like a hologram with strange angles; sharp reds, yellow and greens. So beautiful! I told myself not to pick it up.

But it would prove my story — the shimmering static strong around me, I reached out, just to touch.

Crash — whack! It felt as if the jellybean-thing bit my fingers. In a sudden blinding dazzle I was jerked forward.

Spinning, I plunged deep into those shimmering waves that crashed shut like a hungry mouth.

Blackout.

I woke up, aching and winded. I was in something glass, like a big square bottle, in a huge glossy room that stretched endlessly away.

The glass cage was big enough to stand in, and a sort of seat-shelf ran along the back. On it was a cup of blue liquid and a little plate of yellow pellets. In one corner, on the floor, was a tray filled with purple sand.

A sneery voice called out. "Well, well, no size-limit here, for sure."

Clyde! He was scowling at me from the next cage, through some kind of glass mesh.

Another sneery voice — Bonnie. "Yeah — won't win a prize with that!"

They weren't even freaked! Clyde told me we were in some kind of other world — we'd been reeled in through a dimensional-doorway in the gully. It had been baited to catch something. Like some crazy alien fishing competition.

"They're only after the best!" laughed Clyde. "So how did you get hooked?"

They were both so incredibly up-themselves! They reckoned they'd be celebrities here, as A-class examples of Earth creatures. They didn't need a runt like me around, they said —

A sudden pounding pressure made us all look up.

Out of the glimmery hazy air, something huge came

towards us. I glimpsed a four-legged form, a big eye looking down. A long green arm reached out, bulb-shaped fingers opened my cage door . . . I was gently picked up. Then everything blurred into another crazy tumbling . . .

Tossing head over heels, suddenly I was back in the gully. I rolled over and sat up in the mud. The prickly static closed to a flat line and vanished.

The other world gateway was shut again.

It was still early. I walked home, wondering what I could say. That Bonnie and Clyde had been hooked by some dimensional fisherman? That the gateway had closed again, but maybe it would open in another hundred years?

I did tell my story to the cops. They just said I was freaked out, though a new fence and some "danger" signs went up around the gully.

I remembered Bonnie and Clyde bad-mouthing me about being a runt. Did the "fisherman" hear them? Did he decide to throw me back because nobody likes hooking the little ones?

It's four years since that happened. Bonnie and Clyde are still missing. Maybe they're having a great time in the other world. Maybe not — because there are other things that fisherman do with their catch.

Anyway, I've stopped fishing.

12

The Space Craft, the Parachute, and the Death Ray

Jack Lasenby

"What are you making?"

"A spacecraft."

"What's the Sellotape for?"

"To hold it together."

"Why not use nails?"

"Last time I flew past the moon, I went too close to the Magnetic Mountains. They pulled all the nails out of my spacecraft."

"What happened?"

"I fell to earth."

"Did it hurt?"

"Luckily, I'd taken my umbrella. I used it as a parachute."

"That's all right then."

"No it wasn't."

"Why not?"

"Somebody had cut a hole in the middle of my

parachute, so it let all the air through."

"But you said there's no air in space!"

"Here! Hold this while I stick it together."

"You said there's no air in space . . ."

"There is now. In case of trouble, I'd taken some up in a bottle. I pulled out the cork so the air filled the parachute, and it slowed us down."

"Why didn't the air get away through the hole?"

"I Sellotaped my hanky over it."

"But you'd be upside-down! How did you get the parachute falling the right way again?"

"I told you there's no upside-down in space."

"I forgot."

"Since there's no upside-down or right way up, I just kept falling. I kept falling and saw Earth turning around. I kept falling and saw Italy. I kept falling, the Earth turned, and I saw New Zealand. I did the sums in my head, worked out the right moment, and fired a retro-rocket."

"Where'd you get it from?"

"It was an old sky rocket left over from last Guy Fawkes. I pulled on the parachute ropes and landed on our back lawn. Just by the clothes-line."

"Did you bump?"

"Not much, but it bent the clothes-line a bit. Don't you tell anybody, or I'll fix you!"

"Are you going into space again?"

"When I get this thing Sellotaped together."

"Can I come?"

"No."

"I'll tell them about the clothes-line."

"Oh, all right. Here, hold this while I stick it together."

"How do we take off?"

"Concentration. It's the only way to travel in space. All the other ways need too much fuel. You sit there. Not that one, that's my seat. There! That's it. Now, concentrate."

"What's concentrate?"

"Close your eyes and think hard. Now, hold your breath, and squeeze your nose with your fingers. You mustn't take a breath or we'll come down again. Concentrate! No, don't open your eyes. It breaks the concentration."

"I can't breathe!"

"That's good! It means you're concentrating. All right, we'll give it a proper go. Look out!"

"I haven't got a space helmet."

"Here, you can wear mine."

"That's not a space helmet. That's just a cardboard box."

"Give it back then."

"No, I'll wear it."

"Okay, I'm going to count down. Take a big breath, hold your nose, close your eyes. And concentrate. I'll tell you when you can start breathing again. And remember, don't open your eyes till I say. Ready?"

"I suppose so."

"Ten . . . Nine . . . Eight . . . Seven . . . Six . . . Five . . . Four . . . Three . . . Two . . . One . . . Blast-off!"

"We didn't take off!"

"You didn't close your eyes. You didn't take a big breath and hold your nose. You just sat there and stared. Get out of my spacecraft!"

I'm going to tell them you flattened the clothes-line."

"You tell them, and I'll vaporise you with my death ray."

"What's vaporise?"

"Vaporise is when you fire your death ray and make somebody disappear."

"You vaporise me and I'll tell on you."

"Come back here! All right. Don't say I didn't warn you. Stop, or I'll vaporise you!"

"Yah!"

"I won't warn you again. Here goes with the death ray!"

"Yah! Missed me!"

"Not this time, weasel!"

"Arrrgh! Mum! Mum!"

13

Strange Creatures

Ken Catran

It was midday when the fire-tailed creature came down from the skies. Pyta and Mira normally sheltered from the sun's heat at this time but they were hungry and out looking for food.

"What is that!" muttered Pyta, staring up.

Mira just gaped. Nothing lived up in that red sky. Then the fire-tailed thing slowed and the flames grew less. Suddenly it landed some distance from them.

"I have heard about things like that," Pyta said in a low voice.

So had Mira. The legends that old Boll told of when the sky was blue and the land green. Boll said this sun-baked plain was once something called an "ocean" and full of water. Nowadays water was far below ground where the sun's heat would not turn it to steam.

Ahead the circular thing was still settling on the ground. As they watched, a door opened in the belly and something round slid out.

"It's laying an egg," said Mira hopefully. Eggs were good to eat.

"Eggs don't have wheels," said Pyta.

Now the Egg-wheels thing was rolling in their direction. Pyta shifted his legs because the ridged red plain was always hot; the sun, a glaring red ball overhead.

Egg-wheels kept coming so they squeezed down behind some rocks. These days there were many enemies and food was scarce. It was better to be careful.

Egg-wheels trundled on past then stopped. Had they been seen? Now two strange creatures were getting out of Egg-wheels. They both had silver shimmery skins and their heads were like a huge glass eye. Egg-wheels began moving again, leaving the one-eyed silver-skin creatures behind.

"What are they doing now?" whispered Mira.

Pyta did not know. They were prodding around, putting handfuls of soil into pouches. Why? Everyone knew that nothing grew any more.

"We should get Old Boll," he said.

But Old Boll was far underground with all the family. Nobody came to the surface unless it was to hunt for food.

"They're getting closer," whispered Mira.

But there was nowhere to run. The sun-cracked plain stretched in all directions; they would be seen at once. He and Mira crouched flat. "We shall have to defend ourselves," he said.

She nodded. They waited till the silver one-eyed creatures were close, then suddenly leaped up and cast their nets. The One-eyes were caught by surprise and fell, clutching and grabbing. Pyta and Mira wrapped them up into neat wriggling bundles.

"Come on!" Pyta shouted.

They left the bundled-up One-eyes, ran over to the burrow and down into the cool, winding depths. Boll was in a side-cave with the children around him, telling the old-day stories. Pyta and Mira gasped out their news.

"Creatures from the sky?" Boll shouted excitedly, his joints creaking as he got up. "Show me!"

Pyta and Mira led the way back up the burrow and across the orange-red plain. Boll puffed behind, complaining about the heat. At the rocks Pyta turned, pointing. As he pointed, Mira gasped. Pyta looked and gasped himself as Boll joined them. The two creatures they had left so neatly wrapped were gone. The net-coverings were cut open and empty, and there were fresh marks where Egg-wheels had stopped again.

The sky creature was still there but as they watched, more fire glowed in its tail. It shot up into the sky, became a black dot in the red sky then vanished.

Boll sighed. "The last scientists spoke of sky machines."

Mira picked up something by the cut-open nets. A long sharp little thing like a tooth.

"Ah," said Boll. "That's how they escaped. It's a sort of portable tooth, called a 'knife'. They cut themselves free."

"A portable tooth?" asked Mira puzzled. "Teeth are in the head, claws on hands or feet — who needs a spare one?"

Boll looked at the symbol cut in the handle of the knife.

"Mars," he said. "Before the great fire, we explored other planets. The Martian colony must have built a spaceship to return and check us out. See if there was life left on the planet."

"But they weren't human," said Mira. "They walked on two legs."

Old Boll sighed again. "I must tell you a great secret that should wait until you are older. When too many countries had nuclear bombs — terrible destructive things that killed thousands — they all began using them. The bombs left radiation that would poison Earth for centuries. But spiders were highly resistant to radiation and the last scientists used genetics — to clone humans with spiders. To make a new species of human that would survive."

"And be better!" said Pyta. "Eight legs move faster than two."

"Yes," said Mira. "We can spin our own blanket and catch food in our web. And our poison sting kills enemies so who needs a portable fang? Those two-legged things were the monsters, not us."

"Right," said Pyta. He sat back on six legs and waved his front two in the air, blinking his huge eyes. "Of course, they were fat and well-fed monsters."

Mira's big eyes glowed and her poison sting twitched excitedly. "Perhaps they'll come back and we can invite them to dinner."

Old Boll ran his sharp pointed tongue over his wide mouth. "Yes," he said, nodding happily. "They would taste delicious."

14

Mereana and the Patupaiarehe

Ngahinu Tricklebank

Mereana was the youngest of three brothers and two sisters. They lived with their parents on a dairy farm in the backblocks of the King Country. On one side of the road lay the farm with a river running through it. On the other side was thick native bush often covered in mist, over which hung an air of constant mystery. When their grandmother came to stay, she told them stories about patupaiarehe, those pale, elusive people of another world who were said to dwell in the deepest and highest parts of the forest. Mereana never tired of these stories, and half hoped she might see some patupaiarehe herself, one day.

One morning, Mereana awoke before anyone else and wandered outside. It was about an hour before sunrise and all was still. Mist covered the forest. It stretched in a straight line above the house and continued some distance to disappear in a blanket of fog over the river. As she stood looking up, Mereana heard very faint voices. They gradually grew louder, children's voices, and women's voices, then became fainter. All was quiet again.

The voices had seemed to come from somewhere above her, but there was nothing to see. Mereana was about to tell herself she had imagined it when once more she heard faint voices which gradually grew louder then faded as before. She could not make out what they were saying, but there was a sense of urgency in the women's voices. She was sure now that they came from somewhere above her.

Mereana was more puzzled than afraid, but decided it was time to let someone else know what was happening. She thought immediately of her grandmother Mihiata, who was visiting and sharing her bedroom. Mereana tiptoed through the house. She was surprised and pleased to see Mihiata already up and dressed.

"Haere mai ki waho, e Kui — I've got something very important to show you," she said. And Mereana drew her grandmother outside and showed her the trail of mist above the house.

"Whakarongo, Nan," she whispered. "Can you hear anything? Who are they?"

Mihiata strained her ears and listened. All was absolutely still. Then, very faintly, she too heard the sound of women's and children's voices which gradually became louder until she could make out what they were saying. She listened until the voices faded into the distance then, with a smile, she turned to Mereana.

"Those were patupaiarehe," she said. "Mothers and their children. That trail of mist is their pathway. They travel along it when conditions are ideal."

"What are they saying?" Mereana's eyes were shining.

"The mothers are hurrying their children on, Kia tere tātou tamariki mā, kia tere, kei mau tātou i ā Tama-Nui-Te-Rā. We must be well away from here before the sun comes up, for Tama-Nui-Te-Rā will destroy our highway and we will vanish away with it. Nō reira kia tere tamariki mā." Mihiata paused and smiled as she gazed down at her mokopuna.

"You are a very lucky girl, e moko. Although you did not see them, you heard them, and that is an experience that is given to very few people. What a story you will have to tell your mokopuna!"

Glossary on page 157.

73

15

Three Wishes

Janice Leitch

The old man shuffled down the leafy track, chuckling, for there was mischief on his mind. At last he reached a small pebbly beach. No pebble was as beautiful as the one that sparkled in his pocket. He nudged some stones aside with his boot, and trod the ones underneath into the ground. Next he placed his pebble on top so it could be seen. It twinkled in the sunlight. He stood back in the shadows to see what would happen. He didn't have to wait long.

"Come on, Tama, this is a good place," called Denzil, as he placed his bike against a tree.

"Lovely flat stones," said Tama. "Should be able to skip them right across the stream." He picked one up and spun with his fingers. It bounced four times before sinking.

"I can do better than that!" Prue picked up a large one and spun it across the water.

"Hey, look at this!" shouted Denzil. The old man pulled himself deeper into the shadows, smiling. They'd found it!

"Lemme see!" said Tama.

"Gosh it's beautiful!" said Prue.

"Look, it shimmers," said Denzil, "it must be really precious."

"Wish it was money," said Prue. "I could do with a Big Mac and fries."

Suddenly there was a flash of silver lightning and a deep solid boom.

"Hey, look what I've got!" cried Denzil. He held out his hand. He was clasping a brand-new fifty-dollar note.

"What happened?" asked Tama.

"Magic?" asked Prue.

"Dunno," said Denzil, "but I'll bike off for hamburgers if you like."

"Yes please," said Prue.

"Don't be long," said Tama.

"You were ages," said Prue when Denzil returned wheeling his bike. He handed out the hamburgers, chips and drinks.

"Couldn't help it," grizzled Denzil. "Got a puncture. Wish it could mend itself!"

No sooner had he spoken than there was another flash of light, and a loud boom. Right in front of them, Denzil's wheel spun off the bike. The tyre came off, and the tube, then a patch clamped onto it. Faster still the tube and tyre went back into place, and the wheel was back on the bike.

"Whew, did you see that?" whistled Tama.

"It's been fixed for me. But by who?" asked Denzil.

"Weird things are happening," said Prue. "And I reckon it's the stone you found. Give me another look." She cupped it in her hands and stared. "It's very beautiful, but it looks pretty ordinary to me."

"Hmmf," the old man coughed, and the stone shimmered.

"Is it a wishing stone?" asked Tama.

"No such thing," said Denzil.

"Well, I reckon it is, how else could we get money like that? It just doesn't happen. And look at your tyre getting fixed. It's magic!" said Prue.

"We'd better watch what we say," said Tama. "Weird things sure are happening."

"Like if I was to wish you were a dog, Tama, you'd change into one and chase this stick." Denzil threw a stick into the water. "Wish you were!"

"No, Denzil!" cried Prue.

There was a silvery flash of lightning, more brilliant than before, and a long roll of thunder.

"Woof!" said Tama. The stone went a dull grey colour, but no one was looking at it. "Woof!" said Tama again.

The old man smiled. His work was done. They'd had three wishes. He hobbled along the path. Later he'd return for the stone.

"Quick, wish Tama back," said Prue. "Wish him a boy again. Quickly!"

"I'm trying. I'm wishing like mad. But nothing's happening. The stone is dead. It looks ordinary now, not beautiful like before."

"Forget the stone," said Prue. "How are we going to get Tama back? Here, give it me, I'll do the wishing."

"Woof," said Tama.

"Oh gosh, nothing's happening," said Denzil. "We're in big trouble now!"

"And it's time to go home," said Prue. "Dad said not to be late."

"Come on, Tama," said Denzil. "I don't think Dad will mind if we bring a dog home. I'll hide your bike in the bushes, and you can ride on my carrier."

"You can sleep on Denzil's bed," said Prue.

"Woof." Tama wagged his tail.

"Oh look," said Prue, "just like a real dog."

"Woof," said Tama. He had smelt something in the bushes, and didn't want to go home with Prue and Denzil. It was something that should not have been there. Something mysterious. He was sure it was something to do with him turning into a dog. He had to find out.

But Denzil scooped him up and put him on the carrier. Soon they were on the street where Denzil and Prue lived. "Let's get you inside, before Dad sees you." They stepped into the kitchen just as Dad came in.

"What have you got there?" Dad asked.

"It's a lost dog," said Prue. "Please, may we keep him?"

"Certainly not," said Dad. "He'll have his own home. Put him outside."

"Could we keep him and put an advertisement in the paper?" asked Denzil. "Someone might say they have lost him."

"We are not keeping him, he'd chase the cat," said Dad. "That dog goes outside now."

"But where will he go?" asked Prue. She cuddled Tama.

"Woof," said Tama. He knew where he wanted to go. Back to the stream, back to the track to follow that scent. Back to see what was so mysterious. He pawed at Denzil's pocket.

Denzil put his hand in his pocket and brought out the stone. Tama clamped his teeth round it, almost nipping Denzil's fingers.

"What do you want with that?" whispered Prue.

"Woof." Tama's voice was muffled.

Dad opened the door. "Out," he said, "and don't come back."

Tama trotted down the path. It was a long way to the river without his bike, and by the time he got there it was dark. His feet were sore, and sometimes the stone twitched as though it was trying to jump out of his mouth.

"Where is it? It must be here somewhere!" said a voice close by. Tama could smell mischief. The stone jiggled, and the old man stepped out from behind a tree.

"Ah, there you are," he said. "I see you have my stone. Well, what do you want me to give you for it?"

"Woof, woof." Tama's voice was still muffled.

"Okay then." The old man laughed and snapped his fingers.

The next morning Tama phoned Denzil. "I'm back," he said, "but I'm grounded for a week for getting home late. Tell you about it when I see you!"

"You know," said Denzil and Prue's dad, "that was a very nice dog. Pity we didn't keep him!"

16

The Basket

Adrienne Jansen

There was a kid called Sam. He spoke with little stops and jerks as though the words got stuck between his head and his tongue. He thought that everything was just how it looked.

He watched the old yellow sun slipping below the horizon of the sea and he said, "The sun's fallen into the water."

"No," people said, "it's gone on around the world. It's lighting countries on the other side of the world from us. We just can't see it."

He said, "It's fallen into the water."

At night, he looked up at the stars and he said, "Look at all the new stars."

"They're the same stars as last night, Sam, you just can't see them during the day."

"No," he said in his jerky way, "they're new stars."

One evening he was walking where the flax grew along the curve of the hill. The moon was coming up behind it, a large white moon rolling over the edge of the hill. It shone between the leaves of the flax, and left long threads of light in the dark shadow of the flax leaves.

Sam stopped and looked at the threads of light on the ground. He bent down and rubbed his finger over them. He stood up again, looked at the moon, then laughed.

He walked home quickly. He said, "There's bits of moon on the ground."

"It's just moonlight, Sam. It's where the moon shines on the ground."

"No," he said, "it's long threads. You can pick them up."

People laughed. "Okay, Sam," they said.

Sam took a picnic basket, and walked back across the grass to the curve of the hill. There was the flax and the moon behind it, a little higher now, and the threads of light a little further under the flax, in deeper shadow, but even brighter, as bright as silver.

He bent down and picked one up in his fingers. It was a long bright ribbon of light. It was lying so lightly on the grass that he could lift it like a feather. Gently he laid it in the basket. There was a faint dust of silver on his fingers where he'd held it. He carefully lifted another, then another. Some were tiny slivers tangled among the roots, some were patches like fingernails, some were little flickers he had to skim off the grass with his fingertips.

He laid them all in the basket. The moon rose higher. The ground beneath the flax became all shadow, all the strips of moonlight gone from it.

"I've got enough," Sam said to himself. "I've got a whole basketful." He carefully put the lid on the basket. Through all the chinks in the weave of the basket, there were tiny flecks of light. Sam held it up in the dark and slowly turned it. "Look at that!" he said. "It's beautiful."

He carried it home, and put it in the bottom of his wardrobe beside his shoes. The glow of it spread across his sneakers, and up the shiny sides of his gumboots.

The next day he took the basket out to show to the others. He said, "I picked up all the moonlight from under the flax, and I've got it in this basket."

They looked in the basket. All they could see in the bright daylight were a few pieces of grass and dirt.

"There's nothing there," they said.

"There is. There's moonlight. You just can't see it," said Sam, in his jerky voice.

Someone laughed. Sam shut the basket. He didn't want to show anyone any more. He took it back home, and put it in the bottom of his wardrobe.

That would be the end of the story, except that another kid heard people talking about Sam. "Moonlight in his basket!" they said. "Well, that's Sam."

A few nights later the kid came and knocked on the door of Sam's house.

"Can I see the basket?" he asked.

"What basket? I haven't got a basket."

"Yeah, the one with the moonlight in it."

"Oh that one." Sam put his hands in his pockets. "No, you can't see it."

"Okay," said the boy. "But where did you put it?"

"In my wardrobe." Sam remembered the laughing. "But you're not allowed to look."

But the other kid hung around, and when Sam wasn't looking, he sneaked into Sam's bedroom. He opened the wardrobe door and peered into the black space inside.

There were the sneakers and the gumboots. And the basket. Light was glinting through it, and there was a faint silver glow around it.

The boy drew a deep breath. He knelt down and lifted the lid. And there was all the moonlight, all the long threads and chips and flakes of it, filling the basket up to the brim. He put one finger into it and it felt cold and clear like frost, and the moonlight slithered against itself so that small sparks flew off into the darkness. "It's beautiful," he whispered. He carefully put the lid back on. He wrapped his fingers gently around the curved sides of the basket, and when he lifted them away, there was a faint silver dust on the palms of his hands.

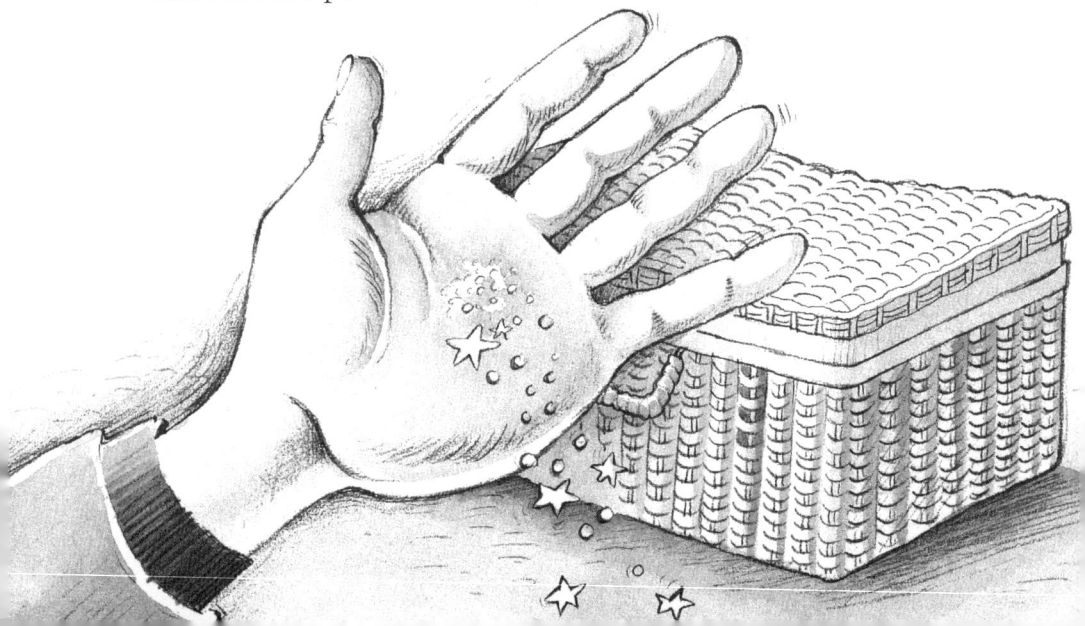

17

Window Shopping

David Hill

The starship hung black and huge above the planet. Inside, Commander X'iv hissed to First Officer X'at. "Search for life forms!"

X'at raised a tentacle in salute. The starship glided across the surface, instruments searching the ground. Photon Deflection Shields made it invisible to anything below.

There is life here, Commander X'iv told himself. Life and slaves.

Far away on the other side of the Milky Way, his planet Y'uk needed slaves to work under the planet's two harsh suns — slaves with limbs to handle machines, and brains to understand and repair them. The search for such slaves had brought the great Y'uk starship to this distant place.

A control monitor flashed. "Life form!" hissed First Officer X'at.

X'iv and X'at watched while sensors probed the forest

83

beneath. Then their scaly heads jerked forward. Across the ground, a long grey-and-brown creature was twisting. A forked tongue flickered. The creature disappeared under a boulder.

"No limbs," X'iv snarled. "Useless for a slave. Continue the search!"

The vast black starship glided on. Below, forest gave way to grassland. The control monitor flashed once more. "This one is fast and strong," First Officer X'at hissed. "See its four legs move over the ground."

On the vid-screen appeared a head with a great mane of fur. It roared at the sky, showing white fangs. A tail swished.

"Just a hunter!" X'iv snarled. "We need creatures with advanced brains. Our planet Y'uk must have slaves. If we find them, we will be rich and famous. If not . . ." X'iv drew a tentacle across his scaly throat. First Officer X'at saluted again — nervously.

On glided the starship. A sea appeared. There was life down there too, with fins and teeth, but nothing that would make useful slaves.

Darkness grew. The starship's infra-red sensors searched on.

"Land ahead, Commander," croaked First Officer X'at. Then he gave an excited hiss. "Lights — thousands of lights! There must be intelligent creatures here!"

X'at was right, his commander saw. Rows and squares of lights covered the surface below. Square buildings stood tall.

"Excellent!" X'iv breathed. "The life forms who made

these are certainly intelligent. But do they have the right sorts of limbs? Close-up focus, X'at!"

New pictures showed. "Look!" X'at sniggered. "Vehicles that still run on wheels!"

Commander X'iv stopped his First Officer with one slap of a tentacle. On the vid-screens, figures passed beneath some of the lights. Then others, moving across flat areas between the bright rows.

"They have limbs!" X'iv hissed. "They walk on their hind ones, and they carry objects with their front ones! These are the life forms we need as slaves!"

First Officer X'at gasped in relief. "Shall I order the rest of our fleet to follow us here, Commander?"

X'iv's yellow eyes grew thoughtful. "First we will capture some, and check their intelligence level."

The invisible black starship crept lower. "There!" hissed First Officer X'at. "Two of them! Standing in that bright square area!"

Commander X'iv's mouth-slit opened in a grin. "Yes — an easy target. Quickly, before they sense us!"

A dazzling blue beam flashed down at the figures in the brightly-lit square. They quivered, then were totally still. The paralysing force-field had worked.

"Come, X'at!" rasped his commander. "We will check these creatures' intelligence ourselves. Keep our Personal Deflection Shields operating. We must not be seen."

The two trapped figures still stood frozen as the scaly shapes of X'iv and X'at crept towards them, invisible behind their deflection shields. Eyes stared helplessly. One figure had a foot lifted to run — too late.

"They have five fingers," snarled X'iv. "Their upper limbs seem strong. Our planet Y'uk has found its slaves! Fit the helmets, X'at. We will make the intelligence test."

From the pack on one scaly hip, First Officer X'at drew two gleaming helmets. He jammed one helmet onto each figure's head. Commander X'iv folded his tentacles across his chest and waited, smirking.

Five minutes later, X'iv was striding in wild circles around the silent pair. His mouth-slit foamed. His tentacles thrashed.

"Fool! Idiot!" he snarled at his terrified First Officer. "It cannot be! The instruments must be wrong!"

"There is no trace of intelligence in these creatures, Commander," whimpered X'at. "Nothing at all."

"Impossible!" shrieked X'iv. "How could creatures who have made these buildings, these lights and vehicles, show no intelligence?"

"Commander," whispered X'at. "Perhaps these creatures are just tools themselves. Perhaps a higher life form uses them as its slaves. Perhaps it is watching us now!"

Commander X'iv's yellow eyes darted at the shadows. "Back to the starship, X'at! For the safety of our planet Y'uk, we must leave here immediately!"

He glared furiously at the two silent, frozen figures in front of him. Suddenly he snatched out his plasma pistol and fired. The figures twisted in flames to the ground.

A few minutes later, the stars above the city were blotted out as a huge black shape skimmed outwards into space, searching for some other planet.

The next morning on Earth was perfectly normal.

Except that in one city, the local TV news had an unusual item.

"Reports of a bright blue flash over a central shopping mall last night," the newsreader said. "Police have no idea what it was. And a strange discovery in a dress shop in the same mall. Two fibreglass models were found burned to ashes inside the display window. The shop-owners say they've never seen vandalism like it."

Starshine

Adrienne Jansen

Every day Mum makes skinny brown sandwiches with tomato and lettuce or Marmite and puts them in my lunchbox. I say, "Not that stuff again!" and she says, "Just eat them. They're good for you." But when she went to Australia to look after Grandad, my uncle Denny came to stay and he made the sandwiches. If Mum had known about Denny's sandwiches she mightn't have asked him to come. Denny made just the best sandwiches! He made great big fat white sandwiches with toast bread, and hundreds and thousands, or chocolate spread, or chips or sliced sausages in them.

The trouble was that all the other kids at school wanted them. They'd look at my fat white sandwiches in the supermarket bag that Denny put them in, and they'd say, "I'll give you my whole lunch for one of them." Or they'd say, "I'll trade you this banana cake for half a one." Sometimes I did swap, but mostly I didn't. I ate my sandwiches by myself, and all the kids gave me slitty-eyed looks as though they wanted me to drop dead. But I didn't care.

Then things started to go bad. Some big boys from the senior school wanted my sandwiches too. The first day they came and sort of stood around and said, "We want your sandwiches." Just then a teacher came over and said, "Move along, boys," and they gave me a bad look and went away. But the next day they turned up again. They came and stood right up close, so that they were shoving me, and they said, "Give us your sandwiches, kid." I managed to duck under their arms and run away, but I was scared.

When I got home from school I talked to Denny. I said, "Your sandwiches are giving me problems."

"How come?"

So I told him. He started to grin. I said, "It's not funny, Denny, they're going to beat me up."

"No they're not. They just need to be taught a thing or two."

That night when he was making my lunch he disappeared off to his room and came back with a tin of something. It looked like shoe polish. When he opened it, it looked like Marmite. But it had lots of little stars in it.

"What's that?"

"Starshine." He had an old toothbrush and he started to spread the stuff on my bread.

"Yuk!" I said, "I'm not eating that!"

"You're right, you're not," Denny said.

I didn't know what he meant. I just watched him wrapping up my starshine sandwiches and putting them in the supermarket bag.

In the morning he said, "Now listen hard."

So I listened hard.

Then I couldn't wait for lunchtime.

At lunchtime I sat down by myself and took out my starshine sandwiches. The sun was shining on them, and the sparkles were all bright and glittery.

"What'ya got there?" The big boys were already on their way over.

I kept pretending to eat my sandwiches.

"What'ya got?" They were standing around me now, really close. I could see all the other kids watching. I felt like I was a boxer in the ring, except that I was the one with no muscles. But I had starshine sandwiches. I just kept pretending to eat them.

"Listen, kid," one of the big boys said. He sounded like he was trying to speak with an American accent. "What's in those sandwiches?"

"Starshine," I said.

"You give me those starshine sandwiches, okay?" There was no teacher anywhere. The big boys were starting to push me around. It was time to give in.

"Okay," I said, "but you have to give me some of your lunch."

They didn't even hear. They'd grabbed my sandwiches, and were in a huddle over by the bike sheds. I tried to see what was happening. Every single one of them was eating my sandwiches. Yay! Better and better.

"Awesome!" I heard them say. They loved that starshine. Then they went quiet. They said things like

"Sththns inmimth." They started putting their fingers in their mouths and poking around in their cheeks. They started to spit the starshine out of their mouths onto the ground. Some of it went on their legs. They all started waving their hands around, and looking at each other's fingers. Now all the other kids could see. Those big boys had warts sprouting out of their fingers! And out of their legs. And they were trying to pull warts out of their mouths.

I took off. I hid in the toilets.

After lunch, the principal called me into his office. "What do you know about this?" He had a bit of bread and starshine in a jar, like a bug.

"I don't know, sir. It was just what I had in my lunch. Some boys stole it."

"They stole it did they? We'll see about that then."

Well, the next day those big boys had to pick up all the rubbish around the school. It took weeks for the warts to fall off, but they left little dark patches like Marmite, and all the other kids called them the Starshine Boys. They hated it!

When I told Denny that night he said, "Serves them right. They got what they deserved." And he started making my lunch, spreading a slice of white bread with starshine. I grabbed it off him. "No way!" I said. "I don't want warts."

"Trust me," he said. And he kept spreading the starshine with the toothbrush.

The next day at lunchtime, I took out my sandwiches. The sun glinted on the sparkles. The other kids stared. "You're not eating that!" they shouted. "Yep!" I said. I shut my eyes. Denny better be right! I took a bite. Those sandwiches were fantastic. They tasted like marshmallow and chocolate ice-cream and chicken nuggets all mixed together. I ate them really slowly. The other kids watched, but they didn't ask for any. They just looked at me like I was weird.

The next day Denny went home. He packed up his tin of starshine and his toothbrush. "Leave some behind so I can show Mum," I said.

"Nope," he said. "It's only for special occasions." Then he gave me a hug. "Don't worry. Those big boys won't bother you again."

They never did. I never had starshine sandwiches again either. Mum came home and I was back to skinny brown sandwiches with tomato and lettuce, but I was so happy to have her back I didn't mind them any more.

"Have you ever heard of starshine?" I asked her one day.

"Starshine? Who told you about that?"

"Denny."

"Oh yes." Mum sighed. "It would be. And I suppose he said it came out of a shoe polish tin, and you put it on with a toothbrush. Don't believe a word of it. It's all just his nonsense."

She winked at me.

19

The Unicorns

Jane Buxton

Over the wild West Coast where strange things happen, a farmer arose very early one morning to drive her cows to market. They were a thin, miserable herd and no longer gave any milk, for she had run out of grass for them.

"Oh, my poor cows," wept the farmer, as she herded them together. "I love every one of you, but there is no grass left and I can't afford to buy hay, so what else can I do?"

Suddenly, out of a ditch hopped a tiny, wrinkled woman dressed all in green. "Because of your great love for your cows, I will help you," she said. And in the blink of an eye the herd of cows became a herd of unicorns, white and sleek, each with a gleaming horn on its forehead. They nibbled on the manuka and swished their long, thin tails contentedly.

"Remember this," said the tiny woman. "Whatever happens, do not forget the great love you have for your animals."

"I won't forget," said the farmer, hugging them in delight. But then she realised she was no better off than before. Although the unicorns had plenty to eat (for they seemed to like manuka better than grass), they were not milking animals like cows. How was she to earn money from her new herd?

Even as she thought about it, one of the unicorns shook its head and its horn fell off. Picking it up the farmer noticed it was hollow and had a small hole in the tip. She put it to her lips and blew. At once the air was full of sounds of mountain streams and waterfalls, bellbirds and tui and high fairy laughter. The unicorns lifted their heads and trotted restlessly along the fenceline.

The farmer took the horn into her workshop and drilled seven evenly spaced holes along it. Now she was able to play it like a recorder. The music was still beautiful, but now it was a tune; it was under control. And the unicorns no longer became restless when she played.

More and more of the unicorns shed their horns and soon the farmer's workbench was covered in horns with holes drilled in them. On some she had even carved little birds and flowers.

On market day the farmer set off towards town with her pack of horns on her back. As she walked she played tunes of the forest, birds and mountain streams. People began to follow her and when she arrived at the market she sold her horns in no time at all.

She returned from town with her pockets bulging with money and her pack full of food. She brought sugar for the unicorns but they just sniffed it and went back to nibbling the manuka.

By the end of autumn all the unicorns had shed their horns and all through the winter the farmer worked on them. She drilled, she carved and she even dyed them different colours.

In the spring she went again to the market and returned with her pockets bulging and her pack full of goodies. She had sold all the horns and had orders for twenty more.

Tiny buds were showing on the unicorns' heads and the farmer waited impatiently for them to grow. She knew if she waited all summer, the horns would be ready in the autumn. But it seemed like a long time to wait and she was running out of money.

She mixed the unicorns a special feed of molasses and barley to help their horns grow, but they wouldn't eat it. She smeared a special ointment on their tiny, budding horns, but they wiped it off on the manuka bushes. So the farmer gave up and spent her time tidying her workshop and sharpening her tools.

Then, one day she noticed the unicorns' horns were growing at last. She began to measure them every day. When most of the horns were about twenty centimetres long, the farmer could wait no longer. "If I cut them off they'll grow again," she told herself. But she couldn't bear to do the job herself. She asked the butcher to come from town with his sharpest saw. And while he cut off the unicorns' horns the farmer stayed inside playing loud music so she couldn't hear their sad cries.

When the butcher brought the horns to her she saw to her dismay that they were not hollow. She tried to hollow them out but the horns were soft and broke easily.

"Oh dear!" cried the farmer. "If only I'd left them until they were ready and fell off by themselves." Then she thought about the unicorns and she remembered the words of the tiny, wrinkled woman — "Whatever happens do not forget the great love you have for your animals . . ."

"I was so greedy for their horns that I *did* forget!" she cried, running out into the paddock. "Oh my poor unicorns!"

Some of the unicorns were lying down, some were standing with their heads hanging low. Where each horn had been was a spot of blood.

"I'm sorry, I'm so sorry," sobbed the farmer. But it was too late to be sorry. The unicorns looked at her with sad eyes and turned their heads away.

The horns never grew again and as each day passed the unicorns became more like cows. They still nibbled on the manuka but they began to eat grass too.

And if you go to the West Coast you may hear strange stories about a herd of very beautiful white cows with no horns. On certain days, the people say, when the West Coast air is filled with the sounds of mountain streams and waterfalls, bellbirds and tui and high fairy laughter, the white cows raise their heads and trot restlessly up and down the fenceline. People who have seen them say they look almost like unicorns.

20

The Virus

Ken Catran

"Crash stations!" yelled Rodar.

The big green planet ahead looked like a wonderful juicy fruit. But its gravity force had suddenly clutched the spaceship like a fist.

"Okay. Under control again," shouted Boomer. She hauled back on the big centre control and the spaceship steadied. "Alon, is the guidance system on line?"

"On line," came the voice of their flight engineer.

The spaceship still shook as though unseen waves smacked against its side. But it was dropping smoothly through the outer atmosphere down to a green and blue surface.

"What an incredible sight . . ." mouthed Boomer.

Below were endless different patches of bright colour. Many greens, both dark and light, joined by winding blue rivers. Yellow too, speckled with different flower colours. They were dropping down to the shores of a huge dark blue lake.

"Magic . . ." breathed Boomer, shaking her fair curls, a big grin on her chubby face.

She had been cloned into life on this spaceship and her first sixteen years of life were enclosed in the cold endless dark of outer space. Now she was suddenly dropping into living colour that she had only seen before in holograms or on a vision monitor.

"Earth must have looked like this," she said softly.

Rodar just nodded. He was programming a landing instruction. He was Boomer's age but dark-haired, scowling with the stress of command. When the automatic controls were set, his frown relaxed.

"It's much bigger than Earth," he said.

Neither had ever seen Earth, of course. They were cloned on this spaceship for the last million kilometres of a voyage that began long ago — billions and billions of light-years ago. They did not even know if there was an Earth any more.

Or, thought Boomer, where the hundred of other spaceships like theirs had gone. Some would have found new planets, their sensors picking up the life-signs. Others would be flying into a black unknown.

Then, "bump-thud" as they settled on the green surface.

Boomer wriggled with fascination. This giant whale-sized ship flew with only a crew of three. Boomer, Rodar and Alon. And of course, SIS, Ship Internal Systems, that had flown them most of the voyage and now settled them gently on land.

"Our voyage is over," she said quietly.

"Maybe," replied Rodar. "Let's see what the scans say."

That clear beautiful air might be poison. Or that sparkling water — even those beautiful flowers. Strange alien beasts might be eyeing them right now. Rodar reset for a quick lift-off. As he did, a strange yowling vibrated through the spaceship.

"What was that?" gasped Boomer.

"Scans say it came from outside," said Alon, joining them. He was small and skinny, with a shaven head and ears that stuck out. "But not animal-related."

Then what is it? thought Boomer. All around, the countryside seemed peaceful. In the distance, a belt of trees shook, but it might have been because of wind.

Now readouts were coming in. Clean air, good soil, minerals, edible nuts and fruit. "No animals," said Rodar, frowning again. "But we can clone those."

In their gene-bank were animals, fish and birds. And people, who would be the architects, farmers and builders in this new planet. Boomer smiled to herself. Maybe they would name the first city after her.

"Can we go outside now?" she asked.

Rodar nodded. They put on their support-suits, just in case. Each also strapped on a laser-pistol before heading into the airlock. Then stopped as the SIS's loud electronic voice sounded around them.

"ADVISE NOT TO GO OUTSIDE."

"Why?" demanded Rodar.

"UNSURE," said SIS. "BAD VIBRATIONS . . .?"

"More like rust in your circuits," snorted Rodar. "Alon, check the programming then join us. This place is as good as it gets."

Alon went. Even so, Rodar and Boomer tensed as the outer airlock opened. But no strange horror waited outside. The sky was deep blue, the air cool and sweet. Ankle-high grass, spotted with red and blue flowers, stretched down to the lakeshore.

A careful look around and they went down the ramp. As they stepped onto the grass, another loud yowl and the ground seemed to shudder. Boomer jumped.

"Earthquake?" she yelled.

Rodar took another step, then another. Nothing else happened and he shrugged. "Ground settling under the spaceship maybe?"

"Found anything, Alon?" said Boomer into her wrist-com.

"Nothing," came the answer. "SIS is still upset so I'm running checks."

Around them were new sounds like strange wonderful music. The wash of water on the lakeshore. The gentle sigh of wind through the trees and the rustle of long grass underfoot.

"What a place," breathed Rodar, smiling for the first time. "And the whole planet is like this. We've found our new home."

Boomer picked a little red flower. It nestled in her silver-gloved hand and she touched it gently. "I wonder if the other ships were this lucky?" Those hundreds of whale-ships who left Earth like theirs, seeking new homes on the other side of the universe. Earth, whose natural resources were gone or polluted; which could no longer support life.

"We won't make the same mistake here," Boomer said aloud.

"We won't get a chance to," came a voice behind her.

Alon was coming down the ramp with a portable scanner. "I've figured out what's happening here."

Boomer took another quick look around. "You're crazy, this place is great! No hostile life-signs at all!"

It's a young planet and living," said Alon. "The way that Earth was once. And giving us fair warning through SIS to get off or be destroyed by earthquakes."

"Why!" shouted Rodar.

"It's frightened," said Alon. "A strange new virus is sweeping through these solar systems. This virus sucks the life from a planet and slowly destroys it."

"We've got state-of-the-art technology on board," said Rodar. "We can help isolate the virus."

"I've done that," said Alon. He rubbed his ears, looking scared.

Now the air seemed chilled and the sky a darker blue. The lake waters lapped coldly as he showed them the scanner readout. It was one that Boomer realised would doom them to more wandering. A single red word that named the virus and explained everything:

HUMANS.

21

Zip Zap Mice

Barbara Else

When Sarah knocked on the door, Aunt Zip opened it. She wore teetery high heels and patchwork pants. "How wonderful!" she cried, and hurried Sarah to the kitchen with her suitcase. Aunt Zap was hanging up a tea towel, wearing tattered running shoes and a long red skirt with black buttons.

"Sarah's come to stay!" Zip cried to Zap.

"Dear Sarah!" both aunts cried. They hugged her and turned her round and round. "Hasn't she grown!" they said. "Isn't she a big girl now!"

Then Aunt Zap shouted, "Bedtime!"

Zip clapped her hands. "Yes! She's a growing girl, and growing girls need their beauty sleep."

"But I just got here," Sarah said. "I haven't had any dinner."

As if she hadn't said a word, Aunt Zap grabbed the suitcase and Zip grabbed her left arm. They hurtled with Sarah out of the kitchen, along a dark creepy passage, up a flight of creaky stairs, and into a little bedroom. The curtains were closed and the bed all ready to climb into.

Aunt Zap dropped the suitcase on the floor. "Breakfast in the morning," she said.

"Of course it's in the morning," Zip said. "Whoever has breakfast at night?"

"I do, sometimes," said Zap. "A bowl of cornflakes, just before I go to bed. It saves time when I wake up."

Zip gave a shriek of excitement. Both aunts raced out of the bedroom and down the stairs again. "Me for the cornflakes! Me for the cornflakes!" they shouted.

Sarah hoped there would be some cornflakes left for her when it really was breakfast time. It was lucky that she had a muesli bar in the suitcase, as well as her pyjamas. She knelt down to open her case. The locks flipped up with a *snip*! *snip*!

There was another *snip*! *snip*!

The room seemed to have an echo. Sarah climbed into her pyjamas and hopped into bed with the muesli bar. As she started to unwrap it, she heard *snip snip* again.

Echoes didn't last that long. She listened, then had a bite of muesli bar.

The *snip snip* came again. Her bed shook a little. Sarah leaned over to see if anything was underneath.

A small skinny monster was crouched there. The *snip snip* was its teeth as it tried to eat the carpet.

"Oh boy!" said Sarah. She reached down and hauled the monster out. It draped over her hand. When she dropped it on the bedclothes, it went *oof*! and began to eat the sheet.

While Sarah had another mouthful of muesli bar, she studied the monster. It was a pretty orange colour, but an ugly shape, rather like a caterpillar. It had six paws, a tail like a bottle-brush, and three feathery bumps down its back.

By now it had eaten a good-sized hole in the sheet and crawled over the pillow to take a bite out of the bed-head — *crack crack*!

A shriek sounded downstairs. Sarah heard her aunts running up in their teetery high heels and tattered running shoes. She popped the monster under her blanket just before Zip and Zap raced back into her room.

"You poor child!" Zip cried.

"You fell out of bed!" cried Zap.

"No I didn't," said Sarah.

"Then what was that noise?" asked Aunt Zip.

"Could it have been mice?" Sarah said.

"Mice! Noisy mice," said Zap. "Sleep tight!" Her aunts ran out and slammed the door behind them.

Sarah pushed back the blanket just as the monster was about to sink its teeth into her toe. "Don't you dare," she told it.

The monster gave a starving groan. She gave it the rest of her muesli bar, which vanished in two gulps.

"Maybe there's something else in my case," Sarah said. She climbed out of bed and found a packet of liquorice allsorts tucked into a pair of clean socks. The monster toppled off the bed like a slinky toy and gobbled up the allsorts very fast.

"None left for me," Sarah said. "You are a greedy pig."

The monster waddled over and began to nibble on the

curtains. *Rip*! *Rattle*! went the curtains on the rail.

"Woops," said Sarah, "here they come again." She grabbed the monster and jumped with it into bed just as Zip and Zap zapped back into her room.

"Mice will chew holes in the wall!" Zip cried.

"Set a trap," Zap said. "Sarah can't sleep with all this noise. Growing girls need their beauty sleep."

Zip stopped flapping around and looked at Sarah. "She's already grown since she got here. Look at that." She prodded the lump in the bed and Sarah leaned over to keep the monster better hidden.

"She's grown a lot," Zap answered. "She can go without her beauty sleep tonight."

The aunts left, more quietly this time.

Sarah set the monster on the floor again. "Where did you come from? I wish you could tell me," she said.

The monster waddled back to the window and stuck its nose up on the sill. It stared out at the moon.

"Did you come from up there somewhere?" Sarah asked.

The monster twitched its bottle-brush tail.

"You ought to go back," Sarah said.

It waggled its tail harder.

"I bet Zip and Zap opened the window to air the room out, and you flew in. When they closed the window, you were trapped."

The monster whined.

Sarah heaved at the window, but it wouldn't slide up. She tried again. Still it wouldn't budge. The monster whimpered. Its nose sunk to rest on its front pair of paws.

"I don't suppose you could chew the window open?" Sarah asked.

The monster's ears perked up. It took a crunch of the wood, and gave a slobber as if it was thinking about the taste. It took a bigger bite. Its teeth *snipped*, *cracked* and *rattled* at the wood. Soon there was a hole in the window- sill, right through to the darkness outside.

"Goodbye, monster," Sarah said, and helped it balance on the edge of the hole.

The feathery bumps on the monster's back spread out into moth-like wings. It launched into the sky and sailed towards the glowing yellow moon, growing smaller and smaller like a paper cut-out as it flew further and further away.

Zip and Zap zapped back into Sarah's room. "Mice! Noisy mice!" they shouted — but stopped when they saw the hole right through the wall.

"Mice?" whispered Aunt Zip.

"Enormous mice," whispered Aunt Zap. "I've never seen such a big mouse hole."

Zip and Zap crept out.

Sarah closed the curtains, climbed back into bed, and giggled till she yawned and fell asleep.

The Day the Water Tank Ran Dry

C. Todd Maguire

For a long time there had been no rain on Waiheke Island.

When the hot wind blew, clouds of dust twirled and swirled along Mere's dirt road. The grass was brown, not green. The ground was cracked and dry.

Piano, Mere's black and white dog, was pleased. No rain meant no bath.

Mere's Mum and Dad were worried. They needed water for drinking and washing and cooking and flushing. The animals needed water, the plants needed water, and the big corrugated-iron water tank was nearly empty.

Mere's Dad tapped the big corrugated-iron water tank with a stick to see how much water was left. But only lightly — so as not to make a hole in the tank.

The water level was very low.

Piano was pleased. No rain meant no bath.

One morning Mere's Dad tapped the big corrugated-iron water tank to see how much water was left. But only lightly — so as not to make a hole in the tank.

The tank was hollow. Dry. Empty.

Piano was pleased. No rain meant no bath.

"What'll we do?" said Mere's Mum. "We need water for drinking and washing and cooking and flushing. The animals need water. The plants need water, and our tank's empty."

"I have an idea," said Dad. "Let's dance!"

Mum and Dad and Mere and Mere's little twin brothers stood in a circle.

Holding hands, round and round, they danced on the dry, cracked, thirsty ground.

The neighbours up and down the street heard the party and beat their feet.

Holding hands, round and round, they danced on the dry, cracked, thirsty ground.

Everyone was having such a good time that they forgot they had no water for drinking and washing and cooking and flushing, and that the animals needed water, and their tanks were empty.

Holding hands, round and round, they danced on the dry, cracked, thirsty ground.

Piano hadn't forgotten there was no water. Piano was pleased. No rain meant no bath.

The sky turned grey.

There was a drop, a drip, a trickle then a spit.

Down Mere's roof the rain came rushing and gushing, swooshing and splashing.

Onto the people the rain came pouring and pattering,

soaking and splattering.

"Yay!" cheered the neighbours. "It's raining!"

And they held out their hands, bowls, pots and pans, for the sparkling cold precious as gold . . .

W A T E R!

23

Getting From A to B

John Connor

"Good morning everyone. Mr Jones is sick today so I'm taking you for Science. My name is Bozokian and I'm from Outer Space."

"Ha, ha, ha," we all laugh.

Jonesy's okay but it's good to have a break from him and Bozokian sounds like he might be fun. He's told us two lies already. No one is called Bozokian and no one is from Outer Space.

"I am stranded on this primitive planet you call Earth." Bozokian sighs and shakes his head. "Help me get back to my planet or I'll be stuck here for ever."

"Where's your spaceship, Sir?" I ask with a laugh and everyone laughs with me.

"Spaceship?" Bozokian laughs back at us. "On my planet such contraptions are in museums of ancient history."

"Where is your planet, Sir?" It's Specky Marsden with his hand up and, being Specky Marsden, he doesn't laugh.

He really wants to know. He really believes Bozokian is from Outer Space. Poor Specky. He's hopeless.

Bozokian looks at the Star Chart pinned up on the side wall and walks across to it. "There." He points at a group of stars near the centre of the Milky Way.

"But that's thousands of light-years away." Specky pushes his specs back up the bridge of his nose. "How can anyone travel that distance?" He might be hopeless, Specky, but he's clever too.

Bozokian reaches into his trouser pocket, pulls out a length of string and stretches it out before us. "On my planet we never travel the distance from A to B." He nods at either end of the string. "We merely bring B to A." He brings the two ends of the string together and puts it back in his pocket.

Specky frowns but I ask the question. "How did you get from your A," I point at the Star Chart, "to our B?" and I nod at the floor.

"A mistake. A miscalculation." Bozokian rolls his eyes. "Do you think I would deliberately choose to come to this uncivilised, barbaric place." After another sigh he walks slowly back to his desk and sits slumped in his chair. "If you help me," he says, "you'll learn amazing things about time and space. If you don't, I'll be stuck here for ever."

So that's what this is about. Time and space. It is a science lesson after all. Still, it looks much more interesting than anything Jonesy would try. I, for one, will go along with it.

"Okay." I look around at everyone else and we all shrug. "We'll help you."

"Good." Bozokian immediately brightens and jumps up from his chair. "Form into four groups of five." He waves his arms and points as we shuffle our chairs and rearrange the desks. That's given him away. He's a teacher all right. Only teachers wave and point and form people into groups.

Bozokian opens his briefcase and pulls out a bundle of metal rods. He distributes them among the groups, all the while giggling to himself as if he's nervous. My group gets three rods. They're extendable, like car aerials only thicker.

"Now then." Bozokian claps his hands and stops giggling though the tendons in his neck tighten and the veins in his temple bulge. "I want you to make a geometric shape with the rods. It could be a triangle, a square, a diamond, a pentagon, anything you like, only hurry." He looks at his watch and out through the window and urges us with: "Hurry or I'll be stuck here for ever."

So, it's a geometry lesson too but, triangles and squares? That's kids' stuff. We did those ages ago. There's a kind of screw attachment at the ends of each rod so, in a minute at the most my group has screwed together a triangle about a metre-and-a-half long on each side. A few minutes more and everyone's finished.

"Now then." Bozokian, whose face is getting redder and redder, claps his hands again. "Bring your shapes out to the front but hurry."

What's the panic? It's just a bunch of shapes, very simple shapes.

"Now put them together." Bozokian clenches his fists and tries to smile at us but it's more like a grimace.

Put them together? He must be joking. They won't fit.

The sides are all wrong.

"Please try." Bozokian pushes and prods us towards the shapes. "I'm sure you can make something."

There's no way we can make anything out of this lot but we all jump in laughing and elbowing each other, pulling and pushing at the shapes. We end up with something that looks like a kid's climbing frame after an elephant's finished climbing on it. There's an oblong flapping about which doesn't fit anywhere.

Bozokian grips his forehead with both hands and groans. "Oh no. I'll be stuck here for ever."

"Hang on." It's Specky again. He takes hold of the oblong, twists it about and fits it together with the other shapes. It still doesn't make any sense and I don't know how Specky did it but there it is. Somehow it all fits together.

"That's it." Bozokian laughs so loud and harsh it's almost a scream. "You've made a doorway." He rushes at it and lines it up with some point in the sky, probably near the centre of the Milky Way. "Oh thank you. Thank you."

There are tears in Bozokian's eyes when I glance at him but I'm too busy staring at the doorway to worry much about Bozokian. There's something inside it, blurred at first but now it's clear. A balcony, and beyond it a vast city of towers and domes. Beyond that a deep blue sky and, filling half the deep blue sky, a crimson planet with thin Saturn rings around it.

When I turn to look at Bozokian he's calm and smiling.

"My home." He nods at the city then goes around shaking our hands and patting our shoulders. None of us say a thing. The most I can do is blink.

After he's finished Bozokian stands before the doorway and raises his hand. "Farewell my friends and thanks again. If you hadn't helped me I'd have been stuck here for ever." He waves then adds with a wink, "As we say on my planet,

The distance from A to B

Is only a step away.

It's easy as ABC

When you bring B to A."

With that he steps through the doorway onto the balcony and disappears along with the balcony, city and planet beyond.

The next day Jonesy is back.

"I hear you had a magician teaching you yesterday." He narrows his eyes at the jumble of rods by his desk. "A very messy magician." He turns his narrow-eyed gaze on us. "Well let me tell you, I'm a scientist. There are no such things as magicians and magic."

"If there aren't," Specky Marsden whispers beside me, "we'll be stuck here for ever."

Trick or Treat

James Norcliffe

Everybody in the street was scared of Mr Withershins, although this was weird because hardly anybody had ever seen him.

He lived at number thirty-nine in an old house which crouched behind a high fence with a high wooden gate which was never opened. Above the fence you could see bits of Mr Withershins' garden, and it was all spikes and pointy things like flax spears and lancewood trees, and while a lot of people in our street had cats and dogs Mr Withershins kept strange animals which made odd howls and squeals like the sound you get when you let the air slowly out of a balloon by stretching its neck.

"Banshees," said Sam knowingly.

"What are banshees?" I asked.

Sam was my older brother and knew a lot of odd words.

"Banshees are what old Withershins has in his garden."

"Yeah, but what are they?" I asked.

"Banshees," said Sam and that was the end of it.

When November came around with Halloween Sam and Amy Leith dressed up as witches with black pointy hats and black cloaks and ghastly lilac make-up. They looked very scary. Sam held an old pillowcase which he hoped to fill with sweets and goodies. They said I could go with them if I didn't get in the way, but that I couldn't expect to get many of the sweets because I had a pathetic costume. I did too. Just an old black jersey of Mum's which hung to my ankles and her old straw gardening hat.

On the night though, I had to do all the dirty work because Sam and Amy were such wimps and wusses. I had to bang on the door and do all the talking while they stood behind looking scary and Amy holding out her hands and Sam holding out the pillowcase.

When we came to old man Withershins' place I was sick of it. All the spears and spikes in the garden were black in the gloomy light and from somewhere behind the tall fence I could hear the weird squealing cry.

"Not going in there," I said.

"Wimp!" said Sam.

"Wuss!" said Amy.

"I am not!" I said. "You two are the wimps and wusses. Who had to bang on the doors? Who had to do the talking?"

They had the decency to look ashamed and they hung their ghastly lilac faces.

But I was angry. "Dare you!" I said.

Sam and Amy looked at each other and went even more lilac. But there was nothing for it. I had dared them.

The gate creaked open and they crept around its edge.

I followed. I was already sorry I'd made them do it.

The path to the front door bent around an old tree. Standing right on the bend was a big bird and even in the gloom its blue was brilliant and it had a great fanned tail with a hundred eyes. It squealed when it saw us and ran off with big awkward steps.

"Peacock!" said Sam.

"I thought you said it was a banshee?"

"No, a peacock," said Sam and he sounded braver.

When Mr Withershins opened the door he looked almost normal apart from his white hair and white beard.

"Trick or treat!" cried Sam nervously.

Mr Withershins looked thoughtful.

"I think I'll have a treat," he said.

Sam shook his head. "No, that's wrong. You're supposed to give us the treat or we play a trick on you."

Mr Withershins shook his head. "Uh uh. You give me the treat or I'll play a trick on you."

That seemed so funny to Sam, he laughed. Big mistake.

"Trick, then," said Mr Withershins. He pointed and there was a blue flash like a hundred flashbulbs and there instead of Sam stood a very surprised looking peacock.

"Aagh!" screamed Amy Leith and turned to run away.

"Trick?" cried Mr Withershins.

He pointed at her disappearing back and there was another flash and all at once instead of Amy there was a peahen scampering around the bend by the twisty tree.

I was really scared but on the ground near the surprised peacock I saw the pillowcase full of sweets. Sam had dropped them when his arms had turned into wings. I

117

snatched them up and before Mr Withershins could point to me I quickly asked, "Treat?"

"Why, thank you," said Mr Withershins, taking the whole bagful. "I'm much obliged . . ."

He gave me a friendly smile and I felt braver. "Would you do a trick for me?" I asked. It was a big risk but I had to try.

"I might," he said, stroking his white beard and smiling.

"Would you turn my brother and Amy back?" I asked. "Please?"

Mr Withershins didn't reply. Instead he pointed at me and the two big birds and there was another blue flash like a hundred flashbulbs. All at once we were standing on the footpath outside number thirty-nine again. From somewhere behind the tall fence I could hear the weird squealing cry.

"Not going in there," I said.

"Wimp!" said Sam.

"Wuss!" said Amy.

I looked at them. It was as though nothing had happened. They couldn't remember.

"I am too," I said. "I'm going home."

"Hey!" cried Sam. "Where's the pillowcase and all the sweets?"

"I gave them to Mr Withershins," I said.

"Don't be such a smartypants," said Sam. "Where are they?"

"I told you," I said.

And I ran home as fast as I could.

25

From Ghoulies and Ghosties . . .

Pauline Cartwright

Years before goldminers came to Otago, Māori regularly crossed through the area on their way to reach West Coast greenstone.

It wouldn't have mattered had the weather been warmer and he'd had some food and dry clothing, but there was a fine rain falling from a cold, grey sky. George's clothes were uncomfortably damp.

He felt in his pockets yet again. No food. His eyes combed the unrecognisable, towering hill slopes. George knew that he had no means of cooking mutton, but had he seen a sheep, it would have meant that some human, somewhere, owned the animal. He would have known the possibility of finding a farmhouse.

The huge, mist-shrouded peaks seemed to be tipping over on him and he began walking again for they didn't seem to tilt so when he moved.

Gently he rubbed the bump on his head. How long

had he lain knocked out at the bottom of the steep slope? Had he been there prospecting for gold? His head ached and his thinking was fuzzy. How long had he been here? And *where* was he?

"Well, I do know I'm George MacPherson, Scottish born." George muttered the words softly. "My memory's clear on that."

Around him the outlines of the hills were dimming as night fell. "I could do with some company. Some company that knew the way back to my camp."

Nearby rocks took on sinister shapes. George gave a short laugh. "Perhaps this is a time to be saying our old Scottish prayer:

From ghoulies and ghosties and long leggety beasties,
And things that go bump in the night,
Good Lord deliver us.

Now why can I remember that, yet not remember why I am here or what I'm doing?"

Dampness was seeping through his clothes, chilling his body. "I wonder if I had a swag? Or a tent? Or was I heading back to camp?"

He could remember camp: the huts and tents, the beginning of a row of flimsily-built shops and the hotels. "My, what I could do for a drink!"

He knew that wasn't really what he wanted. He needed food. His stomach ached with hunger. George staggered a little, stopped, and leaned on a rock. "I should be finding shelter." He spoke loudly trying to thrust aside his fear of maybe dying out here. "I can't even find a river to follow."

Then suddenly, right in front of him, stood a man, a

tall, proud-looking man with hair tied up in a topknot and a fascinating pattern swirling in circles over the contours of his face.

George rubbed his eyes. Gingerly he touched his head again. Perhaps he was starting to hallucinate. The tall man stepped forward. In the half-light, the white of his eyes flashed. George heard a grass-like rustle from the cloak around the man's shoulders.

"You're a Māori, aren't you?"

The man didn't answer.

"I'm lost," George ventured. "Will you help me?"

The man gave no signal that he either heard or understood. Instead, he turned, took a few steps, looked back, and beckoned George to follow.

Hope surged in George's breast. Another human being, who would help him! Of course, he could lead him into a trap. George had heard stories about how Māori sometimes ate people. No. Surely not.

George's feet found new energy. He pushed through the wet tussocks after the man in front of him, followed him round the shoulder of the hill, and found that he was being led along a faint track.

"Why didn't I find this? Do you live hereabouts? Are you mining here yourself?" asked George.

The man turned to make a silencing motion with one hand. He pointed at George's feet, then beckoned again. George did as he was being told. If this man had not turned up, he wouldn't have been able to do it. He would have staggered into the lee of a rock and curled up to nurse his aching hunger, his weariness and fear. If he had slept, maybe he would never have woken. The man in front of him had given him new hope. He would lead him to safety. George knew it.

At least an hour later, over his laboured breathing and beyond the dull ache in his temples, George heard running water. Maybe the sound came from the very river beside which he lived! Perhaps he was nearly back at camp!

As the rain had lessened to no more than a light mist, George smelled smoke wafting through it. He smelled food, and his stomach convulsed with the need of it. Then they came round the bend and he saw two tents. Men moved outside them tending fires. Meat! George could smell meat! He heard it sizzling.

He wanted to run, but he couldn't. Instead he followed his rescuer through the clutching matagouri, up a stone step or two, until he stood in the flickering light of a campfire. George noticed that nobody looked at the Māori and he thought that they must know him well to take so little notice. It was George that the men started towards, seeing the unsteadiness of him as he swayed on his feet, seeing his face white in the darkness. He remembered later that he had turned to thank his rescuer and found him no longer there.

George had only vague recollections of being given hot, sweet tea — and food. Someone removed his wet clothing and wrapped him in dry blankets. He slept.

"I'll take you into town later." He remembered someone saying that to him and realised, when he woke in the middle of the next day, that it must have been one of the men leaving the tent early. Maybe the group was mining out in the hills. He sat up suddenly. Maybe they had made a new, rich strike!

He didn't find out, for Shorty, the man who had spoken to him earlier that morning, returned within the next hour, cooked up another feed which George ate, this time fully aware of each delicious mouthful. Then he threw George his sun-dried clothes and led him away.

"I could find my own way," said George. "I could follow the river."

And maybe, he was thinking to himself, I can get a look at what you men are up to out here in the hills.

Shorty was firm. "I'll take you. I know the shortest way down the old greenstone trail."

"Greenstone trail?"

"The track Māori followed, some years back, when they crossed to the coast collecting greenstone. All this space was theirs, you know, before the runholders and we miners came."

"Aye." George rolled back his sleeves to feel the sun on his arms. It felt so good to be alive, striding between these towering hills, his belly full, his direction purposeful. "I was really sorry I didn't get to thank your Māori mate properly. Will you thank him for me?"

"What Māori mate?"

"The one that found me and brought me into your camp."

Shorty was glancing at George over his shoulder. "We haven't got any Māori mates. No Māori's been on this trail for years. You staggered into camp on your own."

George felt the hair on the back of his neck prickle. He

remembered the way the men had looked only at him and hadn't acknowledged his rescuer. Greenstone trail . . . Māori track . . . from ghoulies and ghosties . . . In his mind, George saw again the tattooed face, the topknot. He *had* seen it.

"Shorty, someone *did* lead me —"

"Don't worry about it, mate. Town's just round the next hill. I'll leave you there, and you can head straight on down."

Shorty swerved slightly to the left as the track forked. George glanced down at the faint trail, the greenstone trail, on the right. A cluster of rocks stood in the distance. Was it a man that stood alongside them? A tall young man?

Shorty strode on ahead. And George scurried to catch up with him.

Mrs Black and the Maths Attack

Pat Quinn

Mrs Black first noticed it on the way home from school. She'd just rounded the corner into her street, when old Mr Green shuffled past. Mrs Black, her arms weighted down by the box of maths books she was carrying, nodded to Mr Green.

"Lovely day, isn't it!" she began loudly. Mr Green was a bit deaf. He gave her a puzzled look, and Mrs Black jumped. The words had come out all wrong. They had sounded more like "Take away fifty-six."

Mrs Black tried again. "Nice time for a walk!" she bellowed.

Mr Green frowned and adjusted his hearing aid. "Five times four what?"

Mrs Black felt a hot embarrassment creep up her neck. She tried to smile, and shrugged her shoulders in a "never mind" sort of way. The box of books tilted dangerously. Mr Green muttered to himself and shuffled on.

"Circle paper," she called, and the hot sweaty feeling turned to a cold shiver. She'd wanted to say, "See you later."

Mrs Black coughed to clear her throat. Maybe she was coming down with the flu.

She reached her gate as the paper girl cycled up. Mrs Black listened for the girl's proud cry of, "Here is your newspaper girl!" but the words she heard were: "Equal to part of the whole!"

Mrs Black shook her head. It didn't help. There was an ominous pattering in her ears like the distant tread of numbers, and her tongue felt thick and heavy. She unlatched the gate and walked up the path.

Mr Black opened the door and smiled. "Thirty metre rule?" he asked.

Mrs Black nodded. It was, indeed, thirsty work at school, and she supposed that's what he had said. The marching thump of numbers echoed through her head.

She dropped the box of books on the floor and wilted into a chair. Mr Black brought in a pot of tea and teacups on a tray. He opened his mouth to speak.

Mrs Black flapped her hands in agitation. She tried to say, "Something's upset me."

"Subtract sixty-three?" repeated Mr Black.

Mrs Black shook her head. She wasn't feeling at all well. "Arithmetic," she said miserably, rubbing her stomach. She pointed to a cup of tea and said, "Divide by three." A shiny tear trickled down her cheek.

Mr Black picked up the cup and looked at it. "Subtract sixty-three, arithmetic, divide by three," he muttered. He leaned forward and peered into Mrs Black's eyes. Then he checked her tongue.

"Mmmm-ha," said Mr Black. He reached into the box of maths books, took out a pencil and pad, and wrote: I THINK YOU ARE HAVING A MATHS ATTACK. He shook Mrs Black's shoulder and showed her what he'd written.

Mrs Black raised one eyebrow. It sank again to join the drooping lines on her face.

Mr Black wrote: YOU NEED SHOCK TREATMENT.

Mrs Black's eyes opened wide and she shook her head, but Mr Black took a deep breath.

"Addition!" he shouted.

Mrs Black sprang to attention, in a sitting position.

"Thirty-three plus twenty-five," cried Mr Black.

"Fifty-eight!" she answered.

"Multiply! Four times twelve!" Mr Black commanded.

Mrs Black saluted and snapped out, "Forty-eight!" and smiled.

"Division!" ordered Mr Black. "Eighteen by three."

Mrs Black began to laugh. "The answer's six!" she giggled.

Mr Black narrowed his eyes and summoned up a line of numbers: "Nineteen minus three plus seventeen minus eight?"

Mrs Black struck them down. "Twenty-five!" she cried.

"How are you feeling now?" he asked.

"Fine!" his wife replied. "I really do feel great."

"I think you're cured," said Mr Black. "Now drink your tea."

"Tea!" groaned Mrs Black. "I forgot to get anything for dinner!"

"You need a rest," said Mr Black. "I'll get dinner."

"Ahh," said Mrs Black. "That would be nice. What are we having?"

Mr Black disappeared into the kitchen and returned looking thoughtful. "What would you say," he said, "to a circle of pizza, divided into eight equivalent parts? Add to that — lettuce leaves, quartered tomatoes and triangles of toast, followed by a rectangle of ice-cream dotted with spheres of hundreds and thousands?"

Mrs Black stretched back in her chair and smiled contentedly. "I'd give it ten out of ten," she said.

The Four Friends
A story from the Solomon Islands

Told by Glorious Oxenham and
Written by Alice Robertson

Four friends lived on a little island in the middle of the
sea. There were a dog, a cat, a crab and a mouse.

One day the dog said, "Let's go fishing!"

They all got into a dugout canoe and paddled out
through the waves, right into shark country.

The dog paddled well with his big paws, the cat paddled
hard with her little paws, and the crab tried hard to paddle
with his claws. All this time, the mouse sat in the back of
the boat, enjoying the ride and doing nothing.

"Why aren't you helping?" the cat asked him.

"My paws are too little," said the mouse.

When they came to a good place, they put out their
lines and waited for the fish to bite. They waited for a long
time in the hot sun, but the fish weren't biting.

"Maybe the sharks have frightened them away," said

the mouse. "I'm bored. Let's have a singing competition."

"I'll go first," said the dog. "I've got the loudest voice."

He sang so loudly and for so long that the cat said, "You're hurting my ears. It's my turn now."

She screeched so loudly that the crab said in his tiny voice, "My turn now."

He began to sing, but his voice was so soft that his friends could not hear him.

"Have you finished yet?" asked the mouse.

"Oh, no. I'm just coming to the good part where my voice goes very nice and high," whispered the crab. He began again.

The mouse was getting bored. He did what mice always do. He began to nibble.

He nibbled a hole right through the bottom of the boat. The cat and the dog didn't notice what he had done because they were straining their ears to listen to the crab.

A little spout of water shot through the hole. The mouse popped his paw in to stop it. The water still came in. So the mouse sat on the hole with his tail dangling down into the water.

Along came a fish and nibbled the mouse's tail.

The mouse jumped up with a squeak. The water rushed into the boat. The mouse's three friends tried to scoop out the water with their paws and claws, but more water kept rushing in, and the boat began to sink.

"Swim!" shouted the dog. He paddled with his big paws. The cat paddled with her little paws. The crab didn't mind because he was used to the water. He just ran along the bottom of the sea. The dog reached the shore first. As he

130

was shaking himself dry, the cat crawled out of the water. Then the crab arrived.

But where was the mouse?

"Our dear little friend," said the dog sadly. "He must be drowned."

The cat began to wail. "Mouse, Mouse," she called. "We love you. Please come back to your friends."

The crab said, "Stop all the fuss, let's look for him."

They looked up and down the beach in the hot sun, but there was no sign of the mouse.

Then the dog said, "I'm too hot to look any more. He must have been eaten by a shark."

"Yes," said the cat. "It serves him right if he's drowned. If he hadn't made that hole, we wouldn't have had all this trouble."

"Quite right," said the crab. "And he wouldn't even listen to my song."

"He was a pest," said the dog. "Let's just forget all about him."

"Forget about me? Forget about ME?" squeaked an angry voice, right in the dog's big, floppy ear. "How can you be so mean? I thought you were my friends!"

The dog looked around. "What was that? It sounded like the mouse, speaking right in my ear."

"More likely water in your ear," said the crab.

"It's not water. It's me — Mouse," came the voice again, in the dog's ear.

"I can still hear it," moaned the dog.

"I'll tell you this," said the cat. "If I ever see that mouse again, I'll grab him in my sharp teeth and gobble him up!"

Right then the dog felt something leap up in his big, furry ear and jump out. It was the mouse, dry as a bone. He had travelled safely to shore in the dog's ear.

Before they could stop him, the mouse was off, running away along the beach with the cat chasing him. Into the distance they went, as swift as light, and for all I know they may be running still.

And from that day to this, cats have *always* chased after mice.

28

The Ebb of the Moon

Jacqueline Crompton Ottaway

Jamie lay awake. Restlessly, he climbed out of bed and gazed outside at the full, fat moon. He couldn't stop thinking about the tree hut that he and his friend John had nearly finished that afternoon. Suddenly he felt a strong urge to visit it, to listen to the waves breaking on the black sands and to enjoy the eerie atmosphere of this bright moonlit night.

Within minutes, he had put on his jeans and warm sweatshirt. Once outside the house, he could see tall cabbage trees silhouetted against the night sky. The beach that lay ahead in the distance, and the hills in the background, seemed to be watching him as he headed along the road past John's house towards the tree hut.

The rough boards of the hut looked solid and strong in the moonlight. Jamie climbed up the steps and squeezed through the doorway. He looked out over the bush towards the beach. The dark green ferns and leaves glinted and

133

shone in the bright slivers of light. Somewhere behind him in the darkness, a morepork hooted.

Ten or fifteen minutes passed before Jamie noticed a strange light flickering on the beach. He peered harder, straining to discover what the weird shape surrounding the light could possibly be. Feeling a little scared, he climbed down from his look-out and started running towards the beach.

As he drew nearer, his amazement grew! Ahead of him, glimmering in the moonlight, he recognised an old timber scow with the gaff-rigged sails that was used for transport around the New Zealand coastline.

His excitement mounted. He had always been keen to have a good look at one of these old boats and now here was one washed up at Piha!

A silver splinter of moonlight moved across the prow of the boat. Jamie gasped. In the flickering funnel of light, he could see strange shapes moving around and he could hear gruff, guttural sounds.

Jamie halted on the sand. Frightened and unsure, he turned to run. Yet, he felt an urgent compulsion to investigate the strange old scow and its mysterious inhabitants.

But this time, as he turned around, he didn't feel afraid. Somehow he felt protected under the brooding hills and the open starry sky. As he moved back, he could see the battered old scow and her passengers much more clearly. It didn't seem possible! He was looking at six rough-shaven and ragged men, their matted hair gleaming in the moonlight.

One of the men uttered a cry, "Come here!" and

beckoned Jamie closer.

"Quickly please. Hurry!" urged the strange voice. Other voices rang out in the darkness.

"Hurry, before it's too late."

"Help us, boy, please."

"Don't be afraid. We won't hurt you."

Jamie took off his sneakers. He began to run. His bare feet crunched along the sand. He didn't feel the least bit afraid now.

"Hurrah, he's coming."

"Good on yer, lad."

"Faster, faster," came the gruff voices. A deep cheer resounded from the boat.

Coarse hands and roughened arms reached out to help him on board. Jamie was still feeling slightly dazed, from the brightness of the moonlight and the discovery of the old beached boat. He found himself staring into warm blue human eyes.

"What's happening —" he began.

"Shussh, boy. We'll explain to you later. There's no time to waste now. Hold on tight! George and Jack, we're ready to move."

Two of the men clambered out and pushed the scow into the tide until the keel was floating freely. Once back on board, they began to tell their story.

"You've no need to be afraid, lad," said a gruff but friendly voice. "I know we're a wee bit terrifying at first, but we won't hurt you. My name's Sam and this is my crew. We need your help."

"But who are you?" interrupted Jamie. "It's all so

strange. You look and dress as though you were living a hundred years ago!"

"I'm not at all surprised that you're confused. You see, lad, we only sail on this old scow once every twenty years when the moon is full and at a certain zenith in the sky," continued Sam as the boat picked up a fresh gust of wind.

"You mean, 'once in a blue moon'," replied Jamie uncertainly, stumbling over the phrase.

"Yes, lad. Once in a blue moon.* For, back in 1872 the six of us were gum-diggers working from Anawhata to Whatipu Beach and living in rough shelters along the coastline."

"I've read about it," Jamie nodded.

"Well," sighed Sam gruffly, "at first we were contented with the simple life. The lure of the yellow gum became like a kind of gold fever in our veins and we all wanted more money. Anyway, the truth was that we became too greedy. So I'm ashamed to admit that we started to plunder the land. Instead of waiting for the giant kauris to be felled first, we lit a fire and razed the hillside near Anawhata so that we could collect our precious gum." He reached deep into his pocket and pulled out a glistening lump of gum. "Here," he whispered, pushing it into Jamie's hand, "hold this, lad, and you'll begin to understand the fever that possessed us."

Jamie looked down at the smooth rounded piece of gum in his hand, gleaming in the moonlight. Carefully, he put it in his pocket.

*A blue moon actually occurs whenever there are two full moons in a calendar month. It is the second full moon.

136

"Aye," added George, "and more's the pity because we've been paying for our deed from that day to this."

"How?" asked Jamie, mystified.

"Mokutuawa, the guardian of Anawhata knew that the fire was no accident. She is a fierce and free spirit and She decided that we must be punished. Mokutuawa placed a curse upon us for our wicked and wasteful ways," George explained.

"And She forced us to sail this scow up and down the coast on a certain brightness of the full moon that occurs about once every twenty years," said Sam sadly. He shook his coarse unkempt head, "Mokutuawa said that we are cursed to remain like this, sailing on this scow up and down the coastline. We shall have no peace until one of our own kind shall rescue us."

"One of your own kind," faltered Jamie, "do you think She would mean an ordinary boy like me?"

The bright blue eyes gazed down at Jamie. "I'm absolutely sure of it, lad."

The wind had freshened considerably and the sails billowed out as the scow sped along. Jamie shivered. He looked at the men around him. They looked so forlorn and forsaken.

Sam leant forward, "You must come with us to Anawhata and plead our case with Mokutuawa."

Jamie sighed. It was a difficult decision. He looked around his strange companions and saw the despair in their faces. At last he spoke. "Yes," he nodded wearily, "I will come with you."

"Hoorah!" came the gruff, guttural chorus.

On the trip around the coast to Anawhata the old boat seemed to fly along. Jamie sat on the deck, listening to the creaking of the timbers, the rustling of the old sails and the surge of the water streaming past the bow. The moonlight seemed brighter and more penetrating than ever, casting ghostly shadows on the worn old scow and its rough and weather-beaten companions. Jamie felt as though he was in another world.

"Wake up, boy. We're here at Mokutuawa's sanctuary. Hurry, it won't be long before the dawn breaks," whispered Sam. "Quickly, we may never find one as brave as you again."

Jamie rubbed his eyes. Despite the fresh sea breezes, he had fallen asleep. "Where do I find Mokutuawa?" he stuttered uncertainly.

Sam smiled gently. "Oh, Jamie. Mokutuawa is a pure spirit. She is Everywhere."

Jamie looked at the kindly, tired men surrounding him. Suddenly he knew that he couldn't let them down. He stood up. "Mokutuawa, Mokutuawa!" he called loudly into the darkness, across the crashing surf. Silence followed. "Mokutuawa, Mokutuawa," he called again, "please listen! These men know that they have destroyed the balance of nature by lighting the bush fires and destroying the forest. But they are truly sorry. Please forgive them," he sobbed, "they have suffered enough."

So still was the silence now that it seemed to ring in their ears. The moon went behind a cloud and an inky darkness descended over the boat. High up in the hills, Jamie heard a low-pitched moan like the whining of the wind. Yet the boat remained perfectly still.

The moon appeared from behind the cloud. Jamie uttered a cry of disappointment. The gum-diggers stood before him, looking exactly the same. Nothing had changed. His cry to Mokutuawa had gone unheeded!

Suddenly the beautiful brilliance of the moon began to fade. Then a powerful eddy of wind swept across the boat. Jamie seemed to be centred in the very vortex of its force. He reached out to touch Sam's shoulder. But he was clutching at empty air. There was no one there. All the gum-diggers were fading and receding into the distance.

Jamie turned with a start as he felt cold water swirling around his ankles. Here he was, back paddling on Piha beach, his sneakers still in his hand. He squinted into the rising sun. There was the faint shape of the old scow, slowly vanishing on the horizon. He felt a hard lump in his jeans' pocket. Slowly, he reached down with his free hand and pulled it out. A golden, molten piece of kauri gum glistened in the soft dawn light.

29

Welcome!

Barbara Else

Odo liked Littletown exactly as it was. He loved picnics on the rolling red hills, especially when the blue daisies were in flower. He enjoyed the beach, where green seagulls sang hello and dive-bombed fish. He liked the lacy metal poles down High Street where lights flared on each evening, orange at first, then fizzing white. He didn't want anything to change.

"You can't always have things your way," Mum said. "Just be polite. The Bell'ohs have come a long way and they'll be tired. We'll have a smile, thank you, not a sour-puss face like that."

The fact was, Odo felt shy. When the Bell'ohs moved in next door he didn't want to look at them, even though he knew folk from Curlie'un all had amazing wings.

The first weekday, Mum told Odo he had to take Bessa Bell'oh to school with him and show her the safest place to cross the road.

"Jeepers creeps," Odo muttered.

"Pardon?" Mum asked.

Odo gave a weak smile. As he walked along with Bessa, he snuck glances at her zigzag wings — they helped Bessa hop over puddles, and dodge the sign for the drycleaner's. At school, some kids gathered round her right away but others, like Odo, were shy and awkward.

When they played scoop-ball, Bessa grew over-excited. Odo had heard what can happen when Curlie'uns become upset. Every so often, the touch of their wings turns things into cheese. Now he saw it for himself. Scoop-ball was no fun when the hoop had suddenly become soft and floppy.

Mr Tomper took the class inside for reading-time, but Bessa was still too excited. Who can read from a book that has cheese pages?

Next thing, Bessa Bell'oh's zigzag wing touched Odo's hair. He yelled. But nothing had happened: Odo was still a normal boy, and feeling stupid. Bessa nudged him again and whispered sorry, she was only curious about the way his hair grew in a topknot.

Odo thought that if she knew where the good places were to play in Littletown, she might leave him alone. So, after school, he showed Bessa the blue daisy bushes where worm-rabbits liked to build their nests. They were both growled at by their parents for being late home.

More newcomers moved into the street down by the sea, the Eepil family, from some place Odo found impossible to spell.

"Don't let me hear you say they're like caterpillars," his father said before Odo had even seen them.

Odo fumed, because he actually liked caterpillars. But the Eepil twins, when they turned up at school, were far worse than Bessa Bell'oh.

It wasn't so bad until Mr Tomper said it was time for gymnastics. Odo was one of the best at gym, and had to admit Bessa was pretty good too. She was helped by those zigzag wings of course. But did the Eepils somersault and vault like everyone else? No. Their idea of exercise was to stand like rolled-up sleeping bags and shimmer while they made a fuzzy noise.

"They're ruining it for the rest of us!" Odo said to Mr Tomper.

"Nothing wrong with being out of the ordinary," said Mr Tomper.

Between fizzes, Lily Eepil said their baby brother could twinkle already and their parents turned all shades of yellow in a brilliant display.

"I'll look forward to seeing that," said Mr Tomper.

How terrible it would be, to glimmer like the Eepils. Odo even hated the way he blushed when he was embarrassed.

That afternoon, his hair turned mustard-colour because Bessa knocked over a paint pot. Odo shouted, she cried, and accidentally turned a desk to cheese. Mr Tomper decided he had better throw it out. Bessa had been so upset that the cheese was growing mould.

Things grew worse and worse, if that was possible. The Sansi-gums arrived, to a house across the road. They had a truckload of round red furniture, two baby Sansi-gums, four children, and a grandad. They liked to sing. Odo heard them start to croon as soon as they slid out of bed on the very first morning. Mr Sansi-gum roared out choruses while he pedalled his red car down to the village. Mrs Sansi-gum did too, as she set about unpacking.

Odo despaired. What would the young Sansi-gums be like at school? As he expected — terrible. He was on playground duty. The new kids huddled together at interval and chanted. They left enormous piles of crumbs. Odo got into a fight with Hushy Sansi-gum about it.

"Give us time," Hushy grumbled as Mr Tomper made the pair of them wipe their noses and straighten their shirts. "We're learning."

"Learning what!" Odo shouted.

"For heaven's sake," Mr Tomper said. "Haven't you paid attention during social studies?"

Of course Odo hadn't. Part of the time he'd been wondering how to catch a worm-rabbit. The rest of the time he'd been counting the hours till the beach concert.

There was one more horrible day at school, with a cheese white-board duster, and more mysterious heaps of crumbs after the Sansi-gum kids stopped singing. And the Eepil twins, instead of joining in a game of four-square at morning interval, stood sputtering like faulty fuses. When it was time for the concert, Odo wasn't in the mood for it at all.

"Stop sulking and enjoy it," his mother scolded.

"No way," muttered Odo.

His parents packed up a picnic dinner anyway. Odo still felt miserable while they spread a blanket on the beach-grass. People of all sorts raced up the red hills and back to

143

use up energy before the concert started. They stuck blue daisies in their hair (if they had any). The seagulls hung around and hoped for scraps.

The mayor welcomed everyone, and there was clapping. Odo's parents rushed on stage first. They imitated characters from TV cartoons until everyone was laughing.

Then Mr and Mrs Bell'oh performed their item. They showed huge bouquets of flowers, which they transformed into different kinds of cheese.

When the Sansi-gum grown-ups had a turn, they sang, of course. But, as they did so, Odo realised their very highest notes began falling back to earth as piles of crackers. Mr Sansi-gum always ended up with big square biscuits, and the grandad with oblongs that snapped neatly into halves. Mrs Sansi-gum's high notes created round wafers with crinkled edges. Hushy caught them in a basket, and grinned at Odo.

The entire Eepil family scrambled on stage for their item, and the mayor ordered the lights to be switched off so everyone would see them better. Their exercises were astonishing, all shades of yellow, orange, dazzling blue-white, and finally purple. The littlest Eepil sat and twinkled at the side.

Everyone exclaimed and cheered and called, "More, more!" Bessa clapped her wings and stomped her feet. Odo found himself applauding too until sparks sizzled off his fingers. Bessa nudged him. He nudged her in return, and laughed.

Then people shared the cheese and crackers. Green seagulls squabbled for the titbits.

"I hear a family called the Fimmers is moving into Little Street," Mrs Bell'oh said to Odo's mother.

Odo thought he'd noticed a Fimmer already. Outside the post shop yesterday, he had seen a kind of pleating in the air. In fact, it might have been two Fimmers. There had been a fold like a smile at about the right height for a grown-up. Lower down, he'd seen a scowl.

It could be interesting at school in the next few days.

30

Out of Sight

Lorraine Orman

Sebastian woke up, reached for his spectacles, and yelped. He peered short-sightedly at the bedside table. A hedgehog bristled back at him. "What?" said Sebastian, jerking upright.

"What yourself!" snorted the hedgehog. "Can I go home now?"

Sebastian heard a muffled laugh from the bed next to his. "Emmanuel," he groaned. "What have you done with my spectacles?"

Emmanuel sat up. So did all the other apprentice sorcerers sleeping in the dormitory. "Feeling a bit prickly this morning are we?" Emmanuel jeered. He waved his wand and the hedgehog vanished in a shower of sparks.

"My spectacles?" Sebastian demanded.

"Oh dear, I've forgotten where I sent them," Emmanuel smirked. "You'll just have to do the Evil Hazards Course without them."

Sebastian's stomach lurched. Emmanuel bullied him because Sebastian always came top of the class. But if he had to do the Evil Hazards Course without his specs he'd fail dismally. "I can't see a thing!" he protested.

"That's the whole idea," Emmanuel chortled.

Sebastian knew there was no use telling their course instructor. A bit of a bully himself, he expected the apprentices to sort out their own problems. Sebastian sent out a locating spell to look for the specs but he knew it would take ages.

Two hours later it was Sebastian's turn to set off on the course. Though he managed to wait until last, his spectacles still hadn't turned up. All he could see of the world was a shadowy blur. "Right," barked the instructor. "Remember, you've only got one gram of magic in your wand. Whoever uses up the least amount of magic is the winner. Off you go!"

Sebastian put his head down. He could only just see the path in front of him. He walked along the path and into the woods, feeling despondent. He'd come bottom of the class for sure.

After walking for a few minutes Sebastian noticed it was getting lighter. He must be coming to a clearing. Ouch! He'd bumped his nose on a large brown something in the middle of the path. It was taller than Sebastian and a lot wider. He started walking round the object but his eye was caught by something glinting on the ground. He picked it up. It was a small glass bottle. He put it in his pocket.

Suddenly a voice like thunder bellowed over his head. "Hoi! You down there! What's up wiv you?"

Sebastian peered round. "Sorry. I can't see you."

"Can't see me?" the voice roared. "The biggest genie in the universe an' you can't see me? You're meant to be scared stupid!"

"Lost my specs," Sebastian explained. He realised the large object in front of him was the genie's boot. What to do? He felt the bulge of the bottle in his pocket, and pulled it out. Maybe, just maybe . . .

"So how you gunna get past me, eh?" the genie thundered.

Sebastian held out the bottle and said a small homing spell.

"Oh, camel's ear!" groaned the genie. "Trust you to find my ruddy bottle." There was a howling tornado and in two seconds the genie had been sucked back into his bottle. Sebastian looked at the spell-o-meter on his wand. He'd only used up a tiny drop of his magic. Excellent.

The pathway came to a rickety bridge swaying over a deep chasm. Sebastian knelt and began to crawl across. There were lots of holes and rotten bits. He carefully placed one hand after another on the crumbling planks.

"Excuse me!" squeaked a voice. "Mind my feet!"

Sebastian peered down a gap and saw a small black creature hanging upside down.

"Sorry," he said. "Who are you?"

"Squadron Leader Rabies of the Ninth Vampire Squadron," the creature squeaked. "We've been dive-bombing you for the last ten minutes. How come you haven't ducked once?"

"Lost my specs," Sebastian said. "I'm as blind as a bat without them."

"Pul-lease," the bat said.

Sebastian apologised.

"So how are we going to tackle you?" the bat piped. "Maybe I should send down our top gun to suck all your blood out?"

Sebastian waved his wand and wrapped himself in a thin protection spell. "Only if he can get through this," he said.

"Oh gnat's nose!" shrilled the bat. "Time to head back to base, lads." And he unhooked his claws from the bridge and swooped away into the chasm. Sebastian looked at his spell-o-meter. It had only gone down a little. "Choice," he said.

Sebastian got through the Valley of Ghosts by keeping his eyes fixed firmly on the pathway in front of him. The ghastly ghosts just looked like swirling mists. The Bog of Monsters was a bit harder but he took his shoes off and felt for the stones of the pathway with his toes. He didn't even notice the monsters slithering and writhing and gnashing their teeth all round him.

The pathway came out of the bog and into the forest again. Sebastian walked on. But then he felt the warmth of sunshine and his ears were suddenly full of sweet music. "Welcome!" called an alluring voice. "You've come so far. You must be hungry and thirsty. Rest awhile at my table and refresh yourself."

Sebastian looked in the direction of the voice but everything was a golden haze. "Who are you?" he asked.

"A harmless water sprite," the voice purred. "My name is Sylvia. Come and sit down. See, all your friends are here waiting for you."

All his friends? The other apprentices? Yeah, right. Sebastian moved his wand a little and put an anti-magic shield in front of him. Then he walked forward over the warm grass.

The first thing he saw was a table laden with delicious food and drink. All the other apprentices were sitting, frozen into statues with food halfway to their lips.

At the head of the table sat a beautiful maiden, with pale skin and blue eyes and long fair hair. "Sit down," she cooed. "Have a goblet of wine."

But Sebastian's anti-magic shield had filtered all the come-hither magic out of Sylvia's voice. "No," he said. "You're a witch!"

"Eye of newt!" Sylvia spat. "Here's a clever one! Well, at least I got most of them. Sorcerers? They're just a bunch of adolescent nincompoops. Used up all their magic before they even reached me."

Sebastian looked at his fellow apprentices and they stared fixedly back at him. He checked his spell-o-meter. It was still three-quarters full. If he carried it on to the end of the hazards course he'd come top. But if he cast a spell to free the other apprentices he'd use up every atom of magic he had left. He sighed. He knew what he had to do. He waved his wand over the bunch of statues.

Sylvia screamed furiously and vanished in a fountain of frothy green water. The boys shook themselves, stretched, and stood up.

"Hey Seb, that was pretty cool," one of them said, looking shamefaced. "We owe you one."

"Too right you owe him, you useless cockroaches!" bellowed the familiar voice of their instructor as he popped out from behind a tree. "Sebastian, you're the only one to pass the course. Your reward is two wand wishes. You know the rules. Use them wisely!"

Emmanuel cringed as Sebastian raised his wand, obviously expecting to be turned into a rat or a slug. But Sebastian sent out a universal command for his spectacles to come back to where they belonged, and suddenly they were perched on his nose. Emmanuel scowled hideously and waited for Sebastian to use the second wish. Sebastian just grinned and turned away. Emmanuel couldn't believe his luck.

But back at the apprentices' dormitory, a very cross, prickly voice could be heard coming from the depths of Emmanuel's bed. "Worm's bum!" it cried. "Not again! Those blasted apprentices!"

Acknowledgements

The publishers gratefully acknowledge the following authors and publishers for permission to reproduce the stories. Where there is no publishing credit, the story is previously unpublished and all rights remain with the authors.

'The Witch's Phone Book', © Rachel Hayward

'Smarts', © Ken Catran

'Tooth', © Peter Friend

'Mr Wardback and the Topsy-Turvy Show', © Sally Sutton

'In the Closet', © Bronwyn Bannister

'The XYZ Files', © Kay Wall

'An Ice Block, Please', © Lorraine Williams, first published in *School Journal,* part 2, no.1, 1980

'Whistle the Wind', © Margaret Beames, first published in *Jabberwocky* 1980 (reworked)

'They Return', © Peter Friend

'Fair Exchange', © Margaret Mahy, first published in *Nonstop Nonsense*, J.M. Dent [Orion Children's Books], 1977

'The Big Catch', © Ken Catran

'The Space Craft, the Parachute, and the Death Ray', © Jack Lasenby, first published in *School Journal*, part 3, no. 1, 1966

'Strange Creatures', © Ken Catran

'Mereana and the Patupaiarehe', © Ngahinu Tricklebank

'Three Wishes', © Janice Leitch

'The Basket', © Adrienne Jansen

'Window Shopping', © David Hill

'Starshine', © Adrienne Jansen

'The Unicorns', © Jane Buxton

'The Virus', © Ken Catran

'Zip Zap Mice', © Barbara Else, Originally published in *Ears*, Random House, 1988 (Reworked)

'The Day the Water Tank Ran Dry', © C. Todd Maguire

Index

Glossary for 'Mereana and the Patupaiarehe'

Haere mai ki waho e Kui — Come outside, Nan

Whakarongo — Listen

Patupaiarehe — the Maori fairy, fair and lifesize

Moko/Mokopuna — Grandchild(ren)

Kia tere tātou tamariki mā, kia tere — We must hurry children , please hurry

Kei mau tatou i ā Tama-nui-te-rā — We must not be caught by Tama the great sun

Nō reira kia tere tamariki mā — So hurry along, children